March 16, 1963

Reflections

On the Nature of the World and Man,
Life's Values and Its Destiny

REFLECTIONS

by

HAROLD E. KOHN

Illustrated by the author

William B. Eerdmans Publishing Company
Grand Rapids, Michigan

This book
is dedicated
by
a grateful neighbor
TO ALL THE PEOPLE OF CHARLEVOIX

A WONDERING-PLACE

UCH has been said these days about the absence of contemplation in our busy world. We moderns are accused by writers, editors, lecturers and preachers of taking too little time for serious thought, for thinking widely, deeply and generously upon the meaning of current events, the boundless potential of man for doing good, the power of human fellowship and co-operation, our individual responsibilities toward the world, our weaknesses and failures, the claims of God upon us, the beauties of creation. Full schedules and overcrowded programs are criticized. A multiplicity of social duties and the countless distractions we find in the realm of entertainment are blamed. We either cannot find time for wondering about the meaning of existence, or if we find time we don't take it.

This criticism of our modern thought-life is just. We do not take sufficient time for careful reflection upon the meaning of life. But I am convinced that we do not find time for thought because we do not find a place for it. We have no wondering-place. Even if we had all the time we wished for silent reflection, we would be unlikely to use it if we did not also find an appropriate place conducive to meditation. Like education and worship, habitual meditation is difficult without a place set aside for it. Perhaps it is possible to gain a splendid education without going to school or college, but in fact few people do so. It is possible to engage in worship outside of a church, but in practice those people worship best outside the church who make a practice of regularly attending a place of worship. We all need a time and a place where we can go with regularity to satisfy our basic needs. Everyone ought to have some place of private meditation — a corner in the attic, basement, or garage if one's home is deep inside the city limits. A country dweller may choose a certain bridge over a certain stream, a big boulder on the lake shore, a grassy mat beneath a great elm, or the shade of a particular birch along a secluded woodland trail. If we are to do any profound wondering we must have a wondering-place.

The wondering-place where I feel most fully alive is Hidden Brook. This forty-acre plot of birch and evergreen forest I have christened "Hidden Brook" because its most endearing feature is a happy little stream, which skips with bubbling excitement and plays hide-and-seek among the flowing skirts of matronly spruce, cedar and balsam.

While water may be inorganic, the brook still seems the most vitally alive creature I have ever met. Never still for a minute, from the time it dashes under our east fence until it rolls under the barbed wire that marks the south boundary of our acreage, the spring-fed stream is a collection of childish moods. It creeps. It crawls. It runs. It laughs up at the balsams, tugs playfully at tolerant cedar roots, and dances around graceful paper birches. It rolls stones along the creek bottom, pushes playfully at the trout, and teases the tamarack, pulling its pigtail tresses. When our neighbor's cattle poke cloven hooves at its sandy bottom, the brook clouds up as if about to give vent to a childish outburst of bad temper. But its hurts are soon forgotten. Its sunny disposition triumphs and its countenance clears again. This dominating little personality, this show-off of a stream, is known on the county maps as Woods Creek. But from the time it hurls itself under our east fence until it whirls under the wires of our south inclosure, it is Hidden Brook to us.

And the loveable little exhibitionist has given the entire forty acres its flavor and its name.

Hidden Brook is our wondering-place. Here the myriad hosts of creeping and crawling and running and swimming and flying things excite the eyes and set thoughts astirring. Here the mind is quickened to fascination by smells washed by gentle breezes to nostrils dilated for exploring the winds. There are tastes here, too, no longer ordinary in our highly civilized world — tastes of running creek water, potatoes roasted in the ashes of an open fire, hamburgers that have sizzled to the touch of open flame and whose juices have drunk deeply of birch and maple smoke. The tangy taste of fruit from ancient, arthritic apple trees, the sweet luciousness of low-growing strawberries, and the subtle wildness of morel mushrooms — these flavors open the mind to new appreciations.

Tall grasses sweep against the wanderer's legs and low-hanging cedar bows whip his shoulders. Tree barks, rough and smooth, invite the touch of an exploring hand. The brook cools tired feet with a tingling chill. Warm sun, pelting rain, stinging sleet, or caressing snow are the weather's greeting to the cheek. These touches of the out-of-doors are nature's partial answers to inquiring minds.

A soft call-note from a clump of birches. What sort of bird is that? At once the mind plunges headlong into a maze of questions from which it might never altogether emerge. A glimpse is caught of a scarlet body carried from birch to cedar on jet black wings. A scarlet tanager, a male! Has the female arrived, too, from the South? Is this bird a transient or a homesteader at Hidden Brook? Where will the nest be? Of what material will it be built? How many young do scarlet tanagers have? Will they live to maturity? What are their natural enemies? Are scarlet tanager babies subject to diseases, like human infants? When do these birds return Southward? These questions and endless others may be kindled by the flash of a tanager's wing.

Every day of the year countless sights and sounds, smells and touches bombard the senses of any visitor to Hidden Brook, and every impact of nature, like flint striking upon steel, can set innumerable questions burning in the mind. Because Hidden Brook is a place of nature's profuse variety of animal and vegetable life, of high banks and low swamp, of somber hills and laughing stream, and of all manner of sensations, it is my favorite wondering-place.

We have done little to Hidden Brook since we purchased the acreage in 1953. We've built Hideaway House there — a two-room study, one room fashioned with both ends almost entirely of glass, a feature which brings the outside inside, and the other room lined with books.

Through the mad tangle of evergreen boughs we have cleared a path along the brook. This we did for the sake of visitors who felt "roughing it" in the out-of-doors need not include being strangled by clutching branches nor smartly slapped by stinging spruce twigs. We have placed some stepping stones across the brook and built a tiny dam of limestone upstream from the cabin. Downstream, by a little natural dam formed by an ancient log, we have thrown in stones to reinforce the decaying barricade nature has formed. Two trout ponds have been dug in a sun-washed glade. We have done little else to Hidden Brook.

But Hidden Brook has done much to us and for us. By just being there, less than ten minutes from Charlevoix, this sanctuary of brook and forest and meadows renders a kindly service. It is the promised rest just beyond exhausting work, the welcome silence beyond the din of civilization, the solitude just on the other side of a world of crowds, the realm of the natural that lies but a step on yonder side of the artificial.

George Tyrrell, the Irish mystic, frequently said that our daily experiences should become the food of our souls. But to make spiritual nourishment of new experiences we must lie down and ruminate on them, much as cows in the field, after eating, lie down and chew their cuds. Tyrrell said that more than half a century ago. It is more emphatically true now. In our fretful search for new experiences we miss the meaning of experiences we are currently having. We buy new records of operas and symphonies before we have absorbed the music we heard last week. We rush through magazines, movies and museums, dash through books, race through country scenes, gulp down new impressions. No wonder we suffer from mental indigestion.

We need time for rumination, for absorption, for turning raw experience into spiritual muscle and sinew. We need time for wondering — and a wondering-place.

May you find your own wondering-place somewhere near.

Acknowledgements

These reflections on life's meaning were written at the author's quiet retreat in Michigan's North Country. They were inspired, not only by the great spruce-cushioned silences of Hidden Brook, where nestles my study on a brook's bank, and by the spacious stretches of sky and water at Wide Sky Harbor, where the Kohn family lives, but by the countless numbers of people who have made their way to these peaceful Northland acres to share with me the questions that perplex them and the problems that plague them. To the Northland, then, to its people, and to those who are its vacation-time visitors, I express hearty appreciation for the stimulation they have brought to me. Traces of their inspiration are stirred into every paragraph of this book.

Members and friends of the First Congregation Church of Charlevoix have cheered me on in my tasks, surely proffering a ministry to their minister far greater than they have received from him. For their generous encouragement I express my thanks.

I am deeply grateful to the Reverends James Sherman and A. Robert Harrison, my partners in the daily work of the ministry at First Church during the writing of this book. Their willing, able and generous assistance has provided me time for the solitude that makes reflection possible.

This book includes essays which first appeared in *The Charlevoix Courier*. The *Courier's* editor, Harold Totten, and his staff have been most kind and heartening. Without them this writing ministry might not have been performed. They have my gratitude.

The essay entitled "A Growing-Place" first appeared in abbreviated form in *The Christian Herald*. I express to Dr. Daniel Poling, editor, my thanks for permission to publish the complete article in this book.

Marian, Carolyn and Larry — my wife, daughter and son-in-law — have been helpful in ways unknown to them. Their genuine interest in my work, their luminous comments and constant encouragement have gladdened and refreshed me, and thus their touch is on all these pages.

The speeding moments carry away our every-day observations of life and its meanings unless somehow our reflections are planted and rooted in today's notations and memoranda. Here are seed-thoughts one man has planted with the hope that someone, somewhere, someday may be nourished on whatever good they may produce, under the blessing of Him who gives the increase.

—HAROLD E. KOHN

Charlevoix, Michigan

CONTENTS

PART TWO
LIFE'S DESTINY

First Book

REFLECTIONS ON THE NATURE OF THE WORLD AND MAN

Part One

WHAT KIND OF WORLD?

1

HOW FAR ARE WE FROM HOME?

ONE of the clearest memories of my early boyhood is
that of our Model-T Ford, with Dad at the wheel,
bumping along the rutted country roads of Michigan's "Thumb" area. The Kohn family was returning
to Flint from any one of many visits to a multitude of relatives
that lived in Sanilac County, Tuscola County, or Genesee
County. I was stretched out with the other children on the
black imitation-leather seat in the back of the car, utterly fatigued
by the exertion of boisterous play with my numerous cousins.
But we were kept awake by the jars and jolts of the inflexible,
unyielding vehicle's lurching over the ruts of unpaved clay roads.
And every few miles one of the youngsters would ask, "How
far are we from home? How far now?"

This is a common question that children ask — "How far
are we from home?" — and we never outgrow the inquiry. Even
now, a third of a century later, whenever we head northward
again after a journey downstate we say to ourselves at frequent
intervals all along the way, "How far are we from home?" "Let's
see now, here we are ten miles south of Grayling. How far
are we from home?" "It's four miles since we went through
Gaylord. How far are we from home?"

3

This homeward pull tugged at John Burroughs' heart when, at eighty-three years of age, he was aboard a train speeding toward the Atlantic Coast from distant California. Burroughs was born in 1837, when Queen Victoria ascended the throne for her long reign as sovereign of the British Empire; now it was 1921, and Queen Victoria's grandson reigned in England. John Burroughs' long life spanned the terms of twenty-one Presidents of the United States, and his years had been loaded with notable activity, investigating the wonders of nature and sharing his nature lore with a vast reading public. But the famed, wise old man had never outgrown the familiar question of childhood, "How far are we from home?" These were his last words. On his trip back East from his California visit, the venerable, white-haired naturalist was stricken ill. When solicitous fellow passengers offered him comfort and help, Burroughs sought from them but one thing — the answer to the question, "How far are we from home?" Then he died.

The question is appropriate for the very young and the extremely old: "How far are we from home?" Where do we stand in relation to where we belong? And if we ultimately belong to a house "not made with hands," if we are not made for a short span of sixty or eighty or one hundred years, to live only in houses made of wood that finally rots or brick and stone that at long last crumble, if we are everlasting creatures

4

who come from and return to an eternal home, then, how far are we from home, our eternal home?

By that question I do not refer to the fragility of life, or to the uncertainty of how long we may have here. We often hear that between the Vice-Presidency and the Presidency of the United States there is only a heart beat. That fact makes life seem fragile and eternity seem close to the most prominent of men, and to us. But the persistent question "How far are we from home?" hints at glad gospel rather than somber warning and reminds us that our faith claims that right now we are very near home. The life eternal is always near us. Heaven is not confined to some remote fenced-off place in a distant sky. Heaven spills over into this life, touching all our common days. The hereafter is also here.

We are now near our eternal home because at this moment we live in the midst of some things that shall never die. Death strikes but cannot hurt eternal things. A traveler in Georgia reports seeing a warning sign on the back end of a huge truck. It read: "This truck has been in 8 accidents and ain't lost any." We know of some things that are even more durable than that truck. They are more secure than civilizations — Egyptian, Babylonian, Greek, Roman, or any of the rest — which seem so permanent but, like last winter's snowflakes, melt and disappear. There are values that outlast the generations of men, who are so hearty-appearing at ten months or twenty years but soon fade away. (Between two and three billion people have been born and have lived and died in the past eighty years.) Even the "everlasting hills" no longer seem everlasting at all since geologists have proven that no sooner are they forced up by some internal upheaval of the earth than they begin to wear down by the erosive forces of wind and water. And the stars, too, fade away, burning themselves out in time so that tonight we shall see the light of some stars that became celestial ashes millions of years ago, but the message of their extinction has

not yet reached us. Civilizations and people, hills and stars meet with final disaster.

But not everything is subject to calamity. The finest influences of those we love most dearly are never lost. We shall always be better because their lives touched ours, and the good we received from them will, in turn, be passed on to those who know us, and from them, in their turn, to still others who know and love them. Like the dew on clumps of blue-eyed grass that is converted into vapor and stirred into the air by summer breezes, and like the moisture coaxed from Lake Charlevoix's tossing surface by the sun's persuasive rays to become part of cloud and rain and freshened earth, good influences are not lost. They go on and on from one life and one place to another. We speak of heaven, our eternal home, as "the life everlasting." But the everlasting things are with us now. As Paul put it, "And now abideth faith, hope, and love." They will always abide. We are not far from home as long as we travel in the area of the things that abide everlastingly.

Moreover, we are accustomed to thinking of our eternal home as invisible to us now. It is beyond the reach of eye or the testing of our touch. But that is almost as true of the Here as it is of the Hereafter. The realm of the invisible is our familiar abiding place.

Where do you live? On Park Avenue, or on Dixon; on the hill, in the valley, in the city, or in the country? In your body? The real you is not the house you live in, or even the body that you inhabit, or in anything that can be measured or weighed or described in terms of color and texture. Your real home is invisible. Your interests and wants, your thoughts and your purposes are where you really live; but you have never seen an interest, a want, a thought or a purpose, but only what these invisible values can do with visible things. We see the birdhouse a boy makes, but the interest in birds and carpentry that prompted him to make it are invisible. A church building is apparent, but the more important things about a church are incapable of being seen. The faith that forms the fellowship of kindred minds, the inner spiritual cravings that bring people to worship remain beyond sensory perception. Houses are seen, but the love that makes a house a home is invisible. We must live in the unseen if we are to live at all, and the more involved we are in the spiritual the nearer we are to our eternal home.

Finally, we are at home with God now if we are ever to be, which is to say we need to practice the fellowship with God we hope to have hereafter. To hope for communion with God and enjoyment of God in "some bright tomorrow" that dawns after death without giving Him time, attention, or love now is like practicing on the mouth organ for fifty years and then declaring, "At the Community Outdoor Concert next Wednesday night I plan to play a piano solo, Rachmaninoff's Prelude in C Sharp Minor!" Well, you won't! Not if your only musical interest has been mouth organs. If you are allowed on the stage at all, the result will not be music but noise. To play the piano well, one must practice piano, not mouth organ. Neither can a person practice indifference toward God all his life and suddenly be ushered by death into joyous fellowship with Him. Such a sudden, unpracticed facing of God would be hell rather than heaven and sheer torture rather than joy. Anyone who practices the presence of God in daily living never gets far away from home, and the final home-going is somewhat of a greatly glorified repetition of what he has done daily — coming into God's presence in great joy mixed with profound humility.

If we are not to be estranged from God and from our eternal home, we must plant a bit of heaven here. A mountain lad once left his log cabin home and traveled to a distant big city to make his living, to marry and rear his family. After thirty-five years he returned to the mountains to visit the ancient, weathered old home and to walk through misty memories of the past. As he slowly sauntered along the creek down by the milk house, he saw a row of tall, stately walnut trees with branches spread in an amber bath of sunlight, and the man remembered how, when he was a very small tow-headed boy, he had brought home from the woods a bag of walnuts and planted them within the sound of the brook's gay laughter. Now there were the trees, silently witnessing to a lad's foresight and adventure.

But what had he done with the rest of those walnuts in the bag? He had not planted them all. Then he remembered: the remainder of the walnuts he had hidden in the attic of the cabin. Now the man wondered if they could still be there.

Small chance. Nevertheless he walked into the long-deserted cabin, found a rickety ladder standing in the cobwebbed corner, climbed the rungs to the hole in the attic floor, pulled himself up, and made his way through tiny jets of light into a far corner. There was the bag, musty and fragile. And there were the walnuts.

The poor, wrinkled, dusty walnuts in his hand and the great trees standing a few yards away, filtering gold from the sun, were of the same age. They once had had an equal chance to make good. But those stuck away in the attic merely existed through wasted years and lost vitality. Only those thrust into the soil had grown into trees and fulfilled their purpose and reason for being.

Our belief in the life everlasting is a walnut-like idea, fruitful only when planted in the soil of everyday life. When stored in written or spoken creed or cleverly reasoned argument, it accomplishes little and gradually loses viability. But when planted in the here and now, the life everlasting springs up, giving the glory of permanence to our daily living, cramming earth with heaven. When we daily live by imperishables, in high fellowship with man and God, enjoying man and God here in partial fulfillment of the greater enjoyment to follow hereafter, deepening our understanding of each other in token of the fuller understanding heaven grants — when we begin the heavenly life on earth — we are certain to live in an abiding awareness that we are never far from home.

2

A REPORT ON SIRIUS

BOUT 8:30 this evening a friend telephoned to say there was a strange light in the southeast, hanging low in the heavens and changing rapidly, a bright light she said. That description fit only one stellar body I could think of. But with all the excitement concerning earth satellites sent up by Russia in the past several months, I wanted to look.

Marian and I stepped outside and, sure enough, there was bold, proud Sirius flashing diamonds and sapphires at earth's dazzled children. We bathed in its beauty briefly and then I phoned our friend and gave her the promised report on our findings.

She wanted to know if it was a star. Yes, it was Sirius, the Dog Star, brightest of all the stars in the heavens. Well, she had never noticed it before. How come? Perhaps, I suggested, it was because the sky is rarely as clear as tonight, and seldom do any of the stars seem so bright.

"But what made the star twinkle so rapidly?" Because its light passes through so much of the earth's atmosphere, which gives somewhat the same shimmering impression that heat does when rising from a hot pavement. The air rising from the

9

sun-warmed surface of the earth distorts the light passing through it.

When I told her that Sirius is about twenty-seven times as brilliant as our sun and very hot, and if it moved as near to the earth as our sun is it would boil away all our oceans, lakes, and rivers in a short time, and that although Sirius is moving in our direction at the speed of four miles per second no noticeable difference in its appearance will be detected by the naked eye for thousands of years, she replied, "How small it all makes me feel!"

"But," I answered, "how big it makes God seem." She agreed.

The smallness of man and the bigness of God are vital parts of the same world-view. If Sirius and its celestial neighbors are at a distance that stuns our imagination, of a magnitude that stupefies our understanding, and if they represent a creative power that dwarfs our own, they not only mock man's smallness but they proclaim God's greatness. They remind us of man's weakness — and of God's might.

Amy Carmichael was a luminous saint who worked so long and effectively among the untouchables of India that her name became a benediction to countless thousands. Much of her radiance and undiscouragable determination she traced to the moment she heard a layman simply pray, "We thank Thee, Lord, that Thou art able."

The stars evoke some such prayer from any thoughtful watcher of the skies — "I thank Thee, Lord, that Thou art able."

3

A GROWING-PLACE

SUMMER days are stimulating, thought-provoking days. We are now surrounded with living, growing things that seem to have a single purpose — to reach fulfillment. Nothing is stagnant. Nothing stands still. All living creatures that are not growing are declining, and all life that is not backsliding is going forward.

From the lowliest to the highest living things, this is a world of latent possibilities. Insects are developing from eggs and larvae that look entirely unlike their parents and are progressing toward the pattern of their kind. No uninformed observer could possibly guess that the pale, white eggs of the luna moth contain potential clear-green caterpillars, or that those caterpillars will some day develop into magnificent, fragile-winged wayfarers on the summer air.

Acorns bear no resemblance whatsoever to oak trees, but they contain possibilities for becoming oaks, and when they respond to the encouragement of fertile soil and to the touch of sun and rain, the vital forces within acorns burst their bonds and grow. First they emerge into the slender grace of saplings, then increase in thickness and height until a single oak is great enough to spread a shade for drowsy creatures of earth, to cuddle bird's nests in their boughs, to drop countless leaves that fertilize the soil, to preserve moisture cupped in its roots and at last, when other services have been rendered, to give its life to make a home and furnishings for man.

In a certain hospital nursery lies a pink morsel of budding humanity for which someone soon will be billed $47.15 a pound, and judged by what the child now *is* the price might seem exorbitant. It bears only the faintest resemblance to a mature person.

11

It has senses, but they are unco-ordinated. It can respond to its environment but only in a random, unorganized way. Its comprehension of the sort of world into which it has come is of the dimmest kind imaginable. But heartening possibilities lie bundled there that should unfold on a predictable growing schedule: a time to smile in recognition, a time to creep and walk and talk. And later there will be a time to learn from teachers and books, a time to decide on a life-mission, a time for courtship and marriage and for children of his own. Nothing in this world is more exciting than a new baby born to parents who deeply desire children, for out of such little miracles God brings big miracles to pass. As Bethlehem reminds us, the greatest forces in the world begin moving when a child is born, and in one helpless-looking Child once stirred the Hope of the world.

The Saviour thought of this life as a growing time and of this world as a growing place. Some of His most memorable parables were about seeds and soil. He told of the wondrous development of a minute mustard seed into a large herb. And again, "A sower went forth to sow," He said, and then described the fate of this seed, depending upon whether it fell on a heavily traveled path, on stony soil, among thorns, or on good ground. (This story, known as "The Parable of the Sower," might better be called "The Parable of the Soils," for it was with growing places rather than seed that Jesus was concerned.) And yet again He said, "So is the kingdom of God, as if a man should cast seed into the ground; and should sleep and rise night and day, and the seed should spring and grow up, he knoweth not how. For the earth bringeth forth fruit of herself; first the blade, then the ear, after that the full corn in the ear."

The parables of growth are rich with many meanings, but it is not a study of these various lessons that we wish to undertake just now. Rather, see the simplest significance of the truth that is common to all of them: this world is a growing place. It is a place full of unrealized possibilities on their way to becoming actualities — seeds becoming herbs of mustard, seeds becoming grain — a whole world of seeds, of beginnings, a world where no living thing is meant to stay as it is. It grows or dies. God's world is a growing place.

I

First, see how the purpose of our basic institutions is reflected in this parable. They ought to be unusually fertile spots in a nurturing world. Our schools should be. A school, whether primary, secondary, college or university, ought not merely to swell a person as a balloon becomes swollen with more air or as a small pond in a rainstorm becomes swollen with more water. It should add quality, as well as quantity, to his living.

Education is not mainly a matter of stuffing young people with more information until their minds fairly burst with facts. Such learning informs without changing the student for the better, making, perhaps, cleverer children out of ignorant children, but little else, letting them remain immature in insight and grasp, in mind and emotion. At its best education changes us. It is primarily an adventure in mental eating where developing minds feed on other minds richer than themselves and from such nourishment sprout into new life and growth.

A good teacher is not one who merely knows his subject. He is a person rich in enthusiasm for study and having abundant affection for students, a person who awakens joy in the pursuit of knowledge and in creative expression, who takes a quiet pride in bearing the name of One who was often called by His disciples "Teacher." A good school is one where the young can find such people in charge. Such teachers see that an educational institution broadens the outreach of young minds, deepens the appreciations of young hearts, whets the appetites of young intellects. Such education matures mind and emotions and leaves the student with valuable left-overs after the facts are forgotten. The intention of education is the education of the intentions, the purpose of education is the education of the purposes, and the heart of education is the education of the heart. When this occurs, schools, colleges and universities give to the world not only better lawyers, engineers, teachers, and scientists, but what the world needs most — young people who have increased in spiritual stature, becoming bigger and better people. Our institutions of learning ought to be and can be growing places.

The home should always be an environment conducive to growth, an extra-fertile spot in a soul-nourishing world. Horti-

culturalists use the word "available" in a most meaningful way. They say a plant food is "available" when it is in such a form that the plant can promptly assimilate it and use it. Some soils contain great quantities of excellent plant food, chemically speaking, but they are in such forms or combinations with other materials that they are almost useless to vegetation. Other soils contain nitrate nitrogen, calcium phosphate or potassium chloride dissolved in water and easily "available" to the plant's hungry roots. Fertile soil is one which contains an abundance of plant food in available form. A good home is more than a place of high idealism and religious belief. It is a seed-plot where growth begins and is encouraged by an abundance of nurturing experiences, where great convictions and high ideals are soluble in exemplary living and available to minds that cannot as readily grasp abstract principles as they can visible deeds. A good home is one where trust in the fatherhood of God is encouraged and made likely by the faithful fatherhood of a good man. In such a home the loving care of the Eternal is made believable by the daily care of the mother, and the brotherhood of man is made real in the relationships of children to each other, all living together in mutual respect, each one valued for what he is and can become, each seeking another's welfare and praying for another's progress and success. When such attitudes are transplanted into the larger world of adult experiences, what a difference they can make! A home is a growing-place, a sort of hothouse where tender souls get their start in a temperature maintained not by hot heads but by warm hearts. If God is to have a better world we need to help Him by improving the conditions in this initial growing-place, the home.

And what of the church? Are our churches growing-places where seeds of the Kingdom find a hospitable home and thrive? Do they transform seeds into "first the blade, then the ear, after that the full corn in the ear"? Or are we relatively unaffected by our churches?

One peril of our religious institutions is that they can be so easily, so subtly, transformed into something other than what they were intended to be, soul-nourishing places. Horace Greeley once received a letter from a woman who was worried about her church, which was suffering a financial crisis. She claimed the members of the congregation had tried every remedy —

suppers and mock marriages, socials, fairs, and festivals — but nothing availed. Could Mr. Greeley suggest a solution? The famed editor replied, "Why not try religion?"

The church can have and should have a place in its program for many activities, but Christians cannot afford to forget that the church of Jesus Christ is a growing-place. There the direction of our growth is changed in conversion so that we cease growing away from God and begin growth toward His likeness. There the pattern of the divine intention for us is placed before us in the person of Jesus Christ, and we are reminded of His stature and fullness by which we measure our progress. There we grow in our capacity for fellowship with God and man, and our little conceptions of God expand into great wonder at God's mercy and grace. We develop in hope, in courage, in dedication and love. In these times when some claim that people must be stronger because the world is getting tougher, it is never enough for the church to insist that people become better and more serviceable. The church must provide a fertile home and place for the assimilation of instruction, inspiration, and power and all the *means* of spiritual development. The church must be a growing-place.

II

Secondly, in this growth-nurturing nature of the world we have a key to some understanding of the place of trouble in human experience. I say *some* understanding, for suffering is not a fathomable mystery while we are here in its midst. Was it not the wisest and the truest of men who prayed in the midst of His agony, "My God, my God, *why* hast thou forsaken me?" Why do *any* of us suffer moments so painful that we feel God-forsaken? The complete answer eludes us. As the dark heavens were mute when Christ flung His tortured cry from Golgotha, so no clear and final answer has been given to the world's troubled — to Job, to Paul and to all the other questioning victims who at last became victors. Yet there is a clue to *one* purpose of suffering in the observation that, while ease withers many a soul, the faith of the troubled often thrives on their afflictions. Not one spiritual leader of the race can be found whose trust did not grow from adversity, and the greatest suffering often has led to the greatest trust. Biographers well know the contribution of crises to character and look not to

16

their subjects' memoirs or press releases for the secret of their achievements but to their crucial hours of disappointment, or illness, or temptations.

Like the sure, inevitable growth of the seeds of God's Kingdom nurtured by the things of earth, the great believer uses all the experiences of life, including trouble, for food and drink. He neglects nothing. When scorching testings come or long-lasting drought, he sends his roots deeper toward the springs of being. From life's fretful delays he draws patience. From failure and success alike he molds humility from discouragement, persistence. From struggle and strain he develops strength, and from grief he grows. reliance upon everlasting things and the Everlasting One.

Forgiveness thrives on trouble. Most of us should be more forgiving than we are. But how does a person get a forgiving spirit? Does God drop it full-grown into the heart? Not at all. "And he said, So is the kingdom of God, as if a man should cast seed into the ground." Not the fully developed fruit, goodness, but the seeds are sown in us. Then conditions of growth must be met. And one of the vital requisites for growth of forgiveness is something and someone to be forgiven. Forgiveness always follows trouble. Our trust in someone must be abused by him before a broken trust can be forgiven, or our kindness must be answered with ingratitude, our gift unacknowledged, our love shunned, our generosity exploited. Without such hurts there could be no healing; without such rebuffs no forgiveness could grow. So when we pray for a more forgiving spirit we are also asking for the trouble that makes forgiveness possible. We cannot hope for the fruit of forgiveness without at the same time becoming vulnerable to the trouble upon which forgiveness thrives.

Or in a moment of insight we see what grumblers we have been, and we pray for more appreciation and gratitude. But how will thankfulness grow in us? Certainly not through receiving more of this world's goods, for material blessings have not thus far kept us from complaint. We may have to lose some of what we possess.

Admiral Richard Byrd, writing of months spent in the Antarctic, told how he left behind at latitude 80° 08' south his vanity and scepticism. But. he brought back to civilization with him something he did not possess before, "appreciation of the

sheer beauty and miracle of being alive, and a humble set of values. . . . I live more simply now, and with more peace." One needs to come close to losing life before one can fully appreciate the thrill of living. We must experience moments or days stripped of life's distracting non-essentials before we can rejoice in simple things. Appreciation seldom thrives in a thicket of plenty. Like a sprouting profusion of garden vegetables, life needs to be thinned out before gratitude, or any of the best things, can grow.

Understanding, too, is evoked by trouble. We all seek a greater measure of comprehension, but it can come to us only when the conditions from which understanding springs arrive with it. Like seed sown in the earth, the power to think deeply and comprehendingly needs conditions hospitable for growth. Problems and perplexities are required. They are indispensable, for the thoughtful mind stretches toward the unexplained as the sunflower turns toward the sun. If understanding of our fellow men is to thrive we shall need those experiences with them that puzzle us and upset our deadly, cock-sure certainties and cause us to review and revise our basic assumptions concerning them. We shall find such experiences in places of friction and disagreement, such as in marriage and the family, in community organizations, and in the arena of international affairs. If understanding is to increase, a time-consuming, spirit-disturbing interest in others will be necessary, because it is by knowing the pitiful history of another failure and shame, sorrow, and suffering that our hostilities are uprooted, making growing room for understanding, compassion, and love. When we seek understanding we seek the trouble which nurtures it.

Dread it as we will, trouble is good for the soul that creatively uses it. Late in the nineteenth century the botanist Julius Sachs demonstrated that the growth of plants increases during the night. But human experience has proven since the dawning of consciousness that the spirit grows most in the darkness. Examine your own life and see how little you have learned from your successes and how much from your failures, how spirit-withering were your moments of ˙glittering self-righteousness and how fruitful were your times of repentance, how unexciting were your moments of solid comfort and how courage-stimulating were your times of dark peril. Trouble is a growing-place.

III

Finally, this should be said: we Christians have our pattern for growth. We know what we ought to become: it is like Him. The possibilities for Christlikeness are within us, often deeply hidden and obscure, but they are there. We are responsible for developing the hidden latencies, and we shall if we are hospitable to the fertile and stimulating experiences of this life and the beneficent downpouring of grace from above. But we must grow to exceed ourselves, not to outdistance others. It is not enough to be better than another, or even than all others, if we still remain less than we could be. The sanest test being given humans today is applied at insane asylums, the test of progress. A person is held there until he is improved. He does not need to be as well balanced as the superintendent of the mental hospital or any other "norm" of sanity, but he must be improved. Wouldn't this be a different world if no one were dismissed from school, or allowed to leave home or church, or released from his trouble until he was better than before — not necessarily to the extent of being as well informed as his teacher, or as mature as his parent, as religious as his minister, or as patient as Job, but better than when he last entered the situation?

We are here in this growing-place to grow. Are you spiritually bigger and better than you were last year? Have you grown since yesterday? How are you doing in your growing-place?

4

WE GAIN BY LOSING

THE principle of sacrifice is built into the nature of the universe. Virtually nothing gets a start here until something else makes room, and nothing lives and grows until something else dies.

Only as old trees yield to disease, lightning, or axe and fall, making an opening for light in the leafy canopy of the forest, do young trees get a start and grow. Only as some individual plants and animals die as food for others can life go on in the universe, for nature is a system of successive incarnations, little worm being eaten by minnow, and minnow devoured by speckled trout, and trout being consumed by man (and the cynic would add, man being eaten by the little worm, thus completing the cycle). The living world is a vast panorama of sacrifices for success, one individual gaining by another's loss. As Goethe said, "Death is Nature's expert device for ensuring abundance of life."

Moreover, everywhere in the world of nature and in the life of man there are abundant illustrations of the principle that every individual gains one kind of success by sacrificing something else. Trees are stationary forms of life, while their plant relatives the tiny duckweeds are mobile, traveling great distances on lake and stream. In the plant kingdom both mobility and immense size have advantages, but a plant cannot have

20

both. So the great plants, the trees, have renounced mobility in favor of strong roots and stability that allow for vast growth and tremendous height and girth. They have gained in dimension and might by losing freedom to move about. Birds that can fly well usually have weak legs, as does the hummingbird. Birds that have strong legs are weak flyers or cannot fly at all, like the ostrich. To gain one power they must lose another. Sacrifice is a built-in feature of this universe.

Religionists have performed mayhem on the word "sacrifice," cutting the joy out of it and wringing it dry of its life-blood of daring and adventure. They have associated the word with anguish and long-faced piety. Sacrifice is not a dry-as-dust act of religion. It is part and parcel of all exciting living, found in the happiest people on their most joyous occasions. Always in our best and most memorable moments we are giving up some one thing that we cherish for something we love still more.

The farmer at work in his field is giving his energy, his thought, his life to the soil and its crops and flocks and herds because he loves his land and the family it supports more than he loves comfort, ease and leisure.

The avid fisherman loves his lures. He carefully ties flies for trout fishing and polishes the plugs and spinners he uses on bass and pike. Baits cost money, time, and effort to obtain and keep in good condition. Yet everyone who fishes expects to lose his lures. When he returns from a trip to his favorite pond or stream the sportsman loves to boast of the whopper that broke his heavy nylon leader and escaped with his best Quill Gordon fly. And any night at fishing camp is incomplete without some old-timer's story of the bass or pike that "stole hook, line, and sinker." We make or purchase a man-made lure or living bait and cast it into lake and stream knowing full well it may get caught on a sunken log, or entangled in a weed bed, or the leader may be snapped by a giant member of the finny tribe. But such sacrifice is all a part of fishing, and we would gladly lose more tackle for the enjoyment we derive from the sport. In fishing, if fun is to increase, bait must decrease. We must lose to gain.

A wedding is one of life's most joyous occasions. Yet the moment of marriage represents a supreme sacrifice and is the beginning of an entire series of sacrifices. The ceremony signifies a revolutionary change in habits of thought and behavior in both bride and groom. All through early childhood the girl and boy were reaching out for things they could possess for their own sakes and their own enjoyment — bottles, rattles, toys. At first everything went into the children's mouths, and later into their pockets and pocketbooks. Gradually the youngsters were taught to think beyond themselves, but until the moment of marriage they were for the most part self-oriented people. Marriage symbolizes arrival at maturity. If bride and groom mean what they say in the ceremony they can no longer be self-seeking. The groom now earns a living for two rather than one. He must think in terms of "our" — our food, our clothing, our shelter, our security. So must the bride. They have sacrificed much freedom. Their freedom to think of self must decrease if the meaning of their marriage is to increase. They must lose to gain. A wedding is a moment of hearty self-giving, as is every important human event.

In the arts, too, we gain by losing. Photography is more than the art of taking good pictures. Much of the effectiveness of a photograph results from careful cropping, cutting off unwanted elements in the picture. The photograph gains beauty

22

as it loses unneeded details. Sculptoring is the art of throwing away excess clay or chipping away excess granite so that the image the sculptor envisioned can stand forth. As the mass of material decreases, the piece of art grows in beauty.

Wisdom consists of knowing what to leave out of life as well as what to include.

Not only is sacrifice natural and good; it is inescapable. Men of the pulpit confront their people with the matter of self-denial as one of choice. We must choose to deny ourselves, they say, if we are to make spiritual progress. That is true, but only half the truth. The fact is we are constantly sacrificing, whether or not we choose to do so. Everyone, the religious and unreligious, the good and the bad, intentionally or unintentionally sacrifices. The best things in life cost dearly but the worst cost supremely. Here is a man, for example, that no one of his acquaintances would think religious. Far from it. He seldom enters the doors of any church and he speaks the name of God more in profanity than in prayer. But he does more self-sacrificing than any saint in history. By unbridled lechery he sacrifices the respect of his family and neighbors — and his self-respect. By continual indulgence of his perverted appetites he mortgages his future health and bankrupts his moral sense so that he no longer can clearly distinguish between right and wrong. By innumerable dishonesties he has made it impossible for anyone to trust him. His frequent disloyalties to family and friends make them suspicious of even his most innocent gesture, so that they not only see through his lying but doubt him when he tells the truth. He is far from a saint, yet he is one of the best examples of complete self-denial I know, for he has sacrificed the best he could have for the worst and the satisfactions of a lifetime for the pleasures of the moment. The self-denial men will practice for the sake of saintliness is nothing compared with the sacrifices they will make for the excitement of a moment!

No one understands human nature or has insight into himself until he sees that we humans are incurably sacrificial. It is a well-known fact in the practice of psychoanalysis that most patients will not regain their mental health if treated for a low fee or for no fee at all, but when charged the regular price (which is considerable) they will respond favorably. There is a need for sacrifice instilled deep in human nature. Regardless

23

of our superficial seeking after something for nothing, there is something deep within us that finds cheapness intolerable and demands that we pay for what we get. In the deeper recesses of the mind we instinctively know that we ought not to gain anything without losing something. And that is one of the finest things that can be said about being human.

5

THE LIGHT-GIVER

A

CANDLE

CAN LIGHT OTHERS

ONLY

WHEN IT CONSUMES ITSELF.

SO WITH ANY SERVANT

OF

THE PUBLIC GOOD:

SPARE YOURSELF,

AND

YOUR LIGHT

GOES

OUT!

6

ONE THING DEPENDS ON ANOTHER

BY mid-September, deer tracks are thick beneath our wind-ravished apple trees. At Hidden Brook countless leaves and many apples have already fallen, and our graceful, white-tailed neighbors frequently cross the moon-drenched meadows to feast beneath the bare-limbed trees, pawing the crisp, crackling leaves aside to find the rosy-cheeked fruit. Although deer are always quite common on these wild acres, every fall we notice an upsurge in their numbers. We strongly suspect that our apples, favorite fruit of the deer tribe, are to be credited with the increased number of white-tailed visitors. And yet, as in other matters, the most apparent causes are not the only reasons for a certain effect. The appearance of more deer is related to rather remote influences. For instance, deer come for ripe apples, but the apples have ripened so beautifully because of conditions existing in the earth around their roots and in the heavens millions of miles beyond the reach of their longest limbs. The natural sugars in the fruit that make apples so palatable and nourishing to deer are stored there through the trees' ingenious chemical use of light from the distant sun. Light energy falling upon the leaves runs the complex apparatus that processes the carbon dioxide the tree absorbs from the air and the nutriments absorbed from the soil by the trees' roots and makes this intake into apples, much as the deer's consumed apples are fashioned by these animals into muscle and sinew.

So the deer tracks coming from all corners of our forty acres and converging upon the wild apple trees at the meadow's edge have something to do with the multi-million-mile-distant sun and the many-millenia formation of the earth's fertile topsoil. In this complex world of nature nothing stands alone, independent of all else. One thing depends upon another.

I have often wished it were easier for people to see how this law of nature is operative in all of life: one thing depends upon another. Nothing stands alone.

We could avoid many a failure if we recognized the interdependence of all things, that every evil is made posssible by other evils and every good thing is dependent upon other good things, and that the best way to avoid a big evil somewhere in the future is to destroy the little evils in the present moment. The most effective way is to do all the good little things we can today, for one thing depends upon another.

Often it has been my plain duty to advise unmarried young people who believe that "heavy petting" is permissible but sexual intimacy is wrong that if the final step is wrong, so are the first steps in that direction. They will not take the final step if they do not take the first. It is not only the great sin that is wrong, but all the little steps that lead to it.

Occasionally a married man has said to me about a serious involvement with "another woman," "I did not intend that it would go *that* far." Of course not. That is the strategy of evil — to point out enticing little paths that detour from the right road and fail to show us their destination.

27

I've known many alcoholics, but I've never yet met one who, upon taking his first drink, said, "Well, here I go . . . headed toward helpless alcoholism."

It is the strategy of evil to masquerade. It knows man is afraid of giants, so evil never mounts stilts and pads itself to appear larger than it really is. Instead, evil stoops and shrinks, disguising itself as an insignificant midget. It incidentalizes itself. Rather than making itself obnoxious and conspicuous by boasting of its strength, it cites its weakness — "See, I couldn't possibly hurt you, could I?"

Many a person who is polite in society is rude and even cruel at home. But no one ever became uncivil and insolent to his marriage partner all at once. Nearly all marriages are happy on the day of the wedding. It is what happens after marriage — the slow erosion of one person's thoughtlessness rubbing on another's thoughtlessness, the wearing of one person's selfishness upon another's. Marriages are seldom destroyed by explosion. Far more often they simply wear thin, little by little, almost unnoticeably, until a sudden strain tears the relationship to rags. We say a ruined marriage is wrong. But then so are all the little discourtesies, acts of selfishness and indifference and grudgefulness that wear on marriages so that love is at last destroyed. Wherever we wish to avoid a big failure we must steer clear of the little failures upon which the big ones depend.

Moreover, the great successes of life depend upon our handling little duties and seemingly insignificant chores well. A stonecutter strikes many a blow with his hammer before he splits a stone in two. It is never the last stroke alone that cleaves the rock, but all the other seemingly futile blows that accomplish his purpose. The successful stroke is dependent upon all the apparently meaningless strokes that went before. The great good deed we hope to do someday will depend upon the quality of all our little deeds performed every day. No carefully made stonecutter's blow is really useless. No human act is wholly without meaning, for everything we do has an effect upon the future.

Everything of earth and heaven in some way or another belongs to every other thing, as a Hidden Brook apple and the light of the distant sun belong to each other.

One thing depends upon another.

7

A WORLD OF MYSTERY:
SOME THOUGHTS ON SEEING A GULL

THE herring gulls have returned to our bay now that the ice is disappearing. With slow, determined strokes they come and mew and cry above these waters. Now they dip and slide upon the winds and gingerly test the water's temperature. They alight upon gently tossing waves and effortlessly float with elegant poise above the amber shallows and out over the green depths. With mincing steps they playfully wade near the shore, and then with sudden, serious decision they rise on beating wings and plunge for fish in deeper water near the pilings. Herring gulls are creatures both of the shallows and the depths.

Gulls are like our human inclination toward wondering. A mind that is alive is prone to deal with the mysteries that stretch in every direction all about us like the great waters beneath a herring gull's wings. Sometimes we deal with the unknown lightly, playfully, and again solemnly. We often say, "I wonder," half jokingly and with a smile, and again with the catch of troubled ignorance and regret in our throats.

Some wondering is merely fanciful, whimsical, and not intended to plumb the depths of life's dim obscurities. It is not a plunge into life's mysteries, but wading and splashing in the shallows. One romps with such questions as these:

Why is the newspaper that is being read by your neighbor on the bus or train always more interesting than the one you hold in your hand?

Why is it that many who brush their teeth each night before retiring seldom bother to brush their minds to remove all corroding thoughts?

Why is it that winter vacations in the South are more enjoyable when we know the people back home are cold and plagued with snow-shoveling and keeping their balance on slippery sidewalks?

Why do those who try too hard to be sweet usually succeed in being merely sickening?

Why does this generation pay the most attention to those whom it will soonest forget, such as idols of the entertainment field?

Why are we more flattered by praise of our secondary traits than by appreciation for our primary gifts, so that a brilliantly intellectual woman prefers to be told she is attractive, and the attractive woman wants to be told she is brilliant, and a man may be prouder of his outdoor cooking than of his administrative abilities?

Why is it that by the time you're wealthy enough to sleep in late you are so old that you wake up early?

Why is it that so few people ever tell the dentist the real reason for canceling tomorrow's appointment?

Why is it easier to drive six miles to hear a sermon than to spend fifteen minutes meditating upon it when you get home?

Why is it so difficult to find a woman who will admit she can "do something" with her hair?

Why doesn't the chronic doubter spend more time and thought doubting his doubts?

Why is it that when men deliberately destroy the works of man we call them vandals, but when they destroy the works of God we call them sportsmen?

Why is it that a college education is about the only thing people are willing to pay for and not get?

Why is it that when men discipline themselves and suffer risks for trophies (as in the Memorial Day Races at the Indianapolis Speedway) we adore them as heroes, but if they sacrifice their lives for God we call them religious fanatics and fools?

Why do we say that one in four marriages fails, when it is just as true and far more hopeful to declare that three out of four marriages succeed?

Such wondering is frolicsome and sportive, more musing than pondering.

Then again the mind moves out beyond wading depth, to where diving deep is possible and swimming is necessary. This is where the more significant questions lie — the problems of character and the meaning of the world and of God:

Why are we so quick to remove something that hurts an eye and so slow to get rid of anything that injures character?

Why are we so much stronger in our oppositions than in our support, louder in condemning what we oppose than in praising what we favor?

Why did the Creator make destruction so easy and creativity so difficult, so that it is easier to bomb a cathedral than to build a tool shed?

Why are some old debauched rascals allowed to live on and on while some great servants of the world die before half their work is done?

Why is God so slow in bringing about peace, if peace is one of His goals and if He is almighty?

Why is there so much senseless suffering in the world if God is good?

It was among such profundities that the minds of many Bible characters plunged. Job asked:

"Canst thou by searching find out God?
Canst thou find out the Almighty unto perfection?
It is high as heaven; what canst thou do?
Deeper than Sheol; what canst thou know?"

Even the doctrines of the Church do not solve the deep mysteries. They hover about them and dip into them as the gulls of our bay poise above the water on beating wings, but they know as little of the greater meanings as herring gulls know of the chemical composition of the water, or the anatomical structure of the fishes that swim here, or the ecological relationships that bind all creatures of the lake together with a chain of interdependence.

Children often resent mystery. They demand immediate answers to their questions. Every "why" should be paired with a satisfying "because —." What are grownups for, if not to solve the mysteries, and pronto? The recognition of our intellectual limitations is a sign of maturity. We still send our curiosities on exciting adventures into the Unknown, but we do not expect them to return laden with complete answers to our deepest questionings concerning the nature of the universe, man, and God. Rather, our inquisitiveness will venture forth like a geologist into a mountain range and it will bring back chips from the rocks. It will not return with the mountain!

Our knowledge is fragmentary, a thing of pieces, a slice of this and a flake of that, bits of facts which when put together never give us the whole picture. Always a piece is missing so that, no matter how much we know, mystery remains. It is now known how many times a black-capped chickadee's heart beats per minute when the bird is asleep (400 times a minute), and the heart beat of an excited canary has been counted (more than 1,000 beats per minute). The breathing rates of common pigeons have been tabulated (450 times a minute in flight, 180 times a minute when walking and 29 times a minute when resting.) Every year hosts of additional facts are discovered about the nature of the world and its inhabitants. But as knowledge advances, mystery deepens. We discover the heart beat frequency for a bird, but does anyone know why the bird was created at all? Our faith may say, "Because God willed it," but that is faith, not knowledge. We know more about disease than ever, but why do we have disease at all? The answer to that question is but conjecture, perhaps reverent guesswork, but guesswork nevertheless.

Concerning the little matters of life we can know a great deal, but about the greatest matters we instinctively feel we know very little. Only fools and the insane are sure about everything. One measure of wisdom and sanity is one's confession of ignorance. It was one of the most scholarly and observant entomologists of all time, Henri Fabre, who said, "Human knowledge will be erased from the archives of the world before we possess the last word about even a gnat." And the wise Chinese scholar of the seventh century, Laotze, declared, "The way that can be expressed is not the Eternal Way. The name that can be expressed is not the Eternal Name."

What, then, should be our attitude toward life's mysteries?

First, we should be grateful for them. Would you want to live in a world so small you could fully comprehend it? Would you want foreknowledge so that nothing came as a surprise? Would you wish a world so superficial and shallow that when you saw the surface you saw everything, like a lake only a fraction of an inch deep? That kind of lake isn't worthy of the name. It is not even a decent puddle! Be grateful for a world deep enough for the mind to swim in!

Secondly, regard the mysterious world as sacramental, pointing to a sacred truth that God's answers are always more wonderful than our best guesses. The earth is not flat, as man first guessed, but round. It does not stand upon a giant turtle's back, as man once thought, but is held by invisible forces in its orbit around the sun. Fossils are not bones planted by the devil to confuse men as our forefathers once declared, but rather indications of an animal kingdom much vaster than we had thought and a world history reaching back further than men's wildest surmises. The stars are not small lights a few paltry miles beyond man's reach as the ancients believed, but enormous torches of burning gases in boundlessly distant heavens, the nearest being 25 trillion miles away. When answers to the riddles of the universe have been found, they have always been more incredibly wonderful than man had dared to guess. Doesn't that raise a hope that the still unknown answers will be as excitingly marvelous, and that God's answers will always be better than our faint hearts anticipate?

Thirdly, keep in mind that all of us already know enough to live better than we are now living. Our problem is not more knowledge but more obedience to the Highest, not more information but more loyalty.

Fourthly, remember that the life of faith is not distinguished by a super-abundance of knowledge about many things, but by a great confidence in a Person. It readily admits, "I do not know," and hastens to add, "But it is known! God knows!"

8

BUT WHAT CAN YOU EXPECT?

A S I sit in my study near the whispering waters of Lake Charlevoix and ponder the abundant life and death around me in tall, aspiring trees and in rotting logs and meditate on human worth, it seems impossible that once upon a time there was no living thing here at Wide Sky Harbor, nothing whatever: no whirring wings of darting redstarts, kingfishers, scarlet tanagers, and many-colored dragonflies, no perch fry and fingerling bass along the shallow water's edge, no rhythmic bending and bowing of wind-lulled birches, no white-tailed dear daintily sipping from the waters that lave their feet. Once

there were no gent-
ly tossing waters to
bathe the shores, no
rolling green hills
that pull up purple
shadow-quilts under
which they slumber
at night. There was
no earth.

If once there was
no earth at all,
whence then all this
beauty and grandeur?
People of faith every-
where believe that
God created the
earth. How He did it,
what techniques and
processes He used,
are causes of wide
disagreement. The most widely accepted scientific theory concerning the birth of this planet is called the "tidal wave theory."
It suggests that far in the past, roughly five thousand million years
ago, some great star came too close to a small star now known as
the sun. This near collision produced a mighty wave of gases
upon the sun. The wave of flaming gases was pulled farther and
farther out from the sun by the gravitational tug of the on-going
star until at last the wave was wrenched away. But as the larger
star receded into the distant heavens, its attraction for the
wave of fiery gases diminished, while the nearer sun's attraction
remained strong. The disconnected strands of gases, parts of
the broken wave, began whirling around the sun, tethered by
the force of gravity, and thus became our solar system of
parent sun and planet offspring. The theory declares that the
gases condensed first into thicker gaseous matter, then into
liquid, and still later into rock. Then followed atmosphere and
water made up of molecules drawn from the vast spaces beyond
the earth, and finally, after countless millions of years, all the
budding and blooming, swimming, crawling, walking, and
flying things of earth we call life.

Science says that this is what apparently happened: earth became the rocky offspring of the distant flaming sun. (And science, with the help of the spectroscope, shows that elements of the earth are the same as those on the sun, just as a torn piece of dress goods may give evidence of belonging to the material and pattern of the original garment.) Faith says if earth originally came from the sun, it did not happen accidentally. God did it. It was His planning, His method of creating, by making first a sun and then smaller celestial bodies from the larger. It is all His handiwork. Science and religion do not conflict here. They but complement each other. Science cleaves to its own activity — analysis of process. Religion holds to its specialty of worth. Science shows us what has been done in nature, and religion claims that what has been done is God's doing, and it is good. Science discovers facts. Religion places a value upon them and interprets them in the light of what one believes about God and His purposes.

The best evidence we have of what God may do with this world and with us is found in what God has already done with the world and with us. This is why religious faith is both retrospective and expectant, both historical and hopeful. Faith looks backward and selects events that are good and meaningful and declares, "God did it," and then looks forward to the good that ought to be and proclaims, "God can do it, because He has already done something just as good and just as great." The history of the Hebrew people is rife with remarkable events which parents recited to their children, incidents showing what man could expect of God. The Almighty had led the children of Israel out of their Egyptian bondage; that kind of deliverance could be expected of God. The people were given a place in a Promised Land of rich fields and great herds of cattle and flocks of sheep. Such good fortune did not happen accidentally; it was God's doing and emblematic of what man could hope for from God.

The cynical are constantly repeating when trouble comes, when human nature shows its flaws, when picnic plans are spoiled by rain, "But what can you expect?" Well, what *can* we expect in this kind of world? For one thing, based on the best evidence we have, we can expect all the rampant earthly glory we shall ever know in nature to arise out of the ashes of a burnt-out mass of spinning gases. We can expect that sort of

36

thing from God. And if that is not "too good to be true," then nothing is. This is what *has* happened under God. It is the sort of thing we can expect Him to do, the seemingly impossible, bringing order out of chaos and beauty out of ashes.

That is a faith I'm holding to in these turbulent days.

Care to join me?

9

IS ANYTHING IMPOSSIBLE?

I

WONDER

IF

ANYTHING

IS

IMPOSSIBLE

TO

A

GOD

WHO CAN MAKE

EVERGREEN TREES

WITH

BLACK TRUNKS

CAST

BLUE SHADOWS

ON

WHITE SNOW!

First Book

REFLECTIONS ON THE NATURE OF THE WORLD AND MAN

Part Two

WHAT MAN IS AND WHAT MAN CAN BE

10

WHERE EARTH AND HEAVEN MEET

FROM where I write I look past our stony beach where sandpipers play and out across gently rippling Lake Charlevoix to the distant emerald shore where rolling hills keep communion with the sky, and I think of many other horizons where earth and heaven meet. Besides that distant union of earth and sky just beyond these inland waters there are countless other horizons where forests rise with a constant urgency toward the sun and stars, where mountains point granite fingers at the heavens, where the timeless sea and eternal sky embrace. Nature abounds with meeting-places. But the most impressive horizon I know of is a creature called "man," in whom earth and heaven meet. In human nature mingle the lowest and the highest elements we know, lust and love, self-indulgence and self-sacrifice, ignorance and knowledge, foolishness and wisdom, bigotry and humility, timidity and courage, the temporal and the eternal.

It is this dual nature of man that supplies one of the chief puzzles of religion and philosophy. The opposites in man are so intimately fused together that is is difficult to find the joints between them. Where does mind leave off and body begin? Even a trained scientist often finds it impossible to

say whether a person's sickness is physical or spiritual, or both. But a veterinary is less apt to have that problem with a beast or a bird. When a cat or a parakeet is sick we do not say of it, "It's all in his mind." We know it's in his body. However, when a boy complains that he's unable to go to school because of a severe headache, but later in the day goes fishing, we conclude his sickness "was all in his mind." But we can never be sure. Where body and mind mingle the point of fusion is uncertain.

Yet we are careful to maintain some distinctions between the physical, touchable, weighable aspects of human nature and the less tangible faculties of our being. If someone dares to say that brain and mind are the same, we challenge him, daring him to make a detailed chemical analysis of the mind in the laboratory as has been done innumerable times with the human brain. We are neither body or mind, but both body and mind. We are neither right or wrong, but right here and wrong there. We are not so much wise or foolish as we are wise in this regard and foolish in another. Man is the meeting-place of weakness and strength, of misery and grandeur, of the dust of the ground and the breath of God.

It is this double aspect of human nature that makes possible either cynical pessimism or half-blind optimism, depending upon which partial view we take — the half-truth that "man is evil" or the half-lie that "man is good." We frequently hear the remark, "Human nature being what it is," and then we are told to expect the worst. "Human nature being what it is, you'll have to look out for yourself first, or you'll lose the shirt right off your back." Or, "Human nature being what it is, it is useless to attempt prevention of war."

Of course, human nature has a powerful potential for evil. It is of the earth, and it is earthy. But that is not the entire truth about human nature any more than the earth is all there is of a horizon. Man, like a horizon, is where earth and heaven meet, where the lowest and the highest come together. And the highest is as much a part of the horizon as is the lowest. If Benedict Arnold, betraying his country at West Point, is demonstrating human nature, so is George Washington, desperately hanging on to hope at Valley Forge in spite of cold and blizzards and the desertion of his troops. If human nature is Al Capone of Chicago making a fortune from vice, human nature is also depicted by Charles Valiant, a French physician, daring to work with X-ray before scientists had learned to protect themselves from those powerful rays, but refusing to quit his important research although his fingers had to be removed, and later his arm at the elbow, then his arm at the shoulder and at last his other arm. If human nature is John Wilkes Booth firing a bullet into Lincoln's brain, human nature is also Abraham Lincoln giving his life for the Union. So when someone points to the evil man does and cynically

45

asks, "But what can you expect of human nature?" I am inclined to counter, "You can expect George Washington, or Charles Valiant or Abraham Lincoln." As the book of Genesis puts it, "The Lord God formed man of the dust of the ground and breathed into his nostrils the breath of life; and man became a living soul." Earth is present in man, and heaven too. Dirt is there, but so is Deity. The realist does not take his choice between the two and form a philosophy from his preference. He recognizes both.

The irresponsible expressionists miss the real moral significance of the twofold nature of human beings. The expressionists exclaim, "Enjoy yourself, it's later than you think," and advise the unrestrained acting out of every feeling and the fulfillment of every bodily urge. But sensualism and libertinism are no more the manifestations of what is in man than is prayer, or self-denial, or holiness. Meanness is no more evidence of what is in man than is magnanimity. Man is selfish and sacrificial, little and great, sensual and spiritual. Man is a horizon where earth and heaven meet. When, therefore, the expressionist gives full vent to the worst that is in him, the earthly, and represses his possibilities for good, the heavenly, he is less than half a man as surely as this little earth represents far less than half of what is out there on the distant horizon where a small world meets the greatness of the sky.

Express yourself? I should say so! You are body. Take care of it. Feed it. Exercise it. Work it. Rest it. Express it purposefully, wholesomely, in a way that will not shame you before God or man. But you are soul, too. And the soul should govern and hallow the body as the heavens dominate and bless the earth which gets its energy from the parent sun, and its light, and its rain, and its gravitational pull, and its direction — all from above.

Great manhood and womanhood is where earth and heaven meet, and heaven wins.

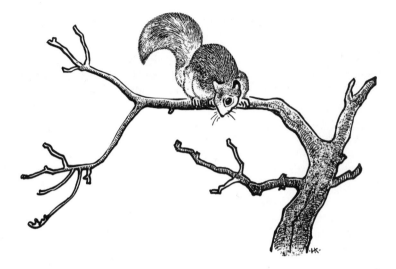

11

ON BEING FIT FOR LIVING

A CHIEF wonder of the natural world is the fitness of things. If living creatures cannot find an environment that suits them, they change to fit their environment. If circumstances are not to their liking, they accommodate themselves to unsatisfactory circumstances. If difficulties cannot be avoided, they develop ways of mastering their difficulties.

While watching fox squirrels bound from ground to tree trunk and from limb to limb, I have often marveled at their sure-footedness. Seldom does a squirrel slip and fall. Possibly life would be more to a squirrel's taste if Nature had treated him with more consideration; growing nuts on the ground in convenient piles so that climbing for them would be unnecessary. Then squirrels could go to the convenient supply and eat their fill. No strenuous, perilous climbing would be necessary. But since Nature doesn't suit a squirrel's convenience, the squirrel has become adapted to Nature's demands. Its leg and ankle bones are so swiveled as to make the fox squirrel agile among vertical tree trunks and swaying limbs. Its claws are long and strong for gripping bark. Its tail is fluffy and parachute-like for easing an occasional fall. Its sense of balance is unusually keen and is aided by its tail, which it uses as a tightrope walker uses an umbrella to help him cross a taut rope. The squirrel's environment is not ideal, but the animal has made the most of it.

To hear the bobwhite quail chant his cheery song from a stump or fence post one would think he was wholly without care and worry. But he has concerns enough, and his short, wide wings are reminders of the quail's hazardous way of life. Unlike the herring gull and tern, whose wings are built for slow but sustained flight and day-long food-seeking, a quail's wings are designed for quick bursts of speed from his enemies, among which are the fox, the bobcat and the domestic cat. Being a ground feeder, thriving on beetles, weevils, grasshoppers, and crickets, spiders, snails, ragweed, corn, wheat, beggarweed and cowpeas, tender leaves and fleshy fruits, the bobwhite is vulnerable to attack while at his meals. But he is ready for escape, outfitted with a keen sense of hearing, sharp eyes, and those wings that beat the air with a whistling velocity.

Biologists tell us that animals and birds were not always as they are now. As environments changed, they, too, slowly changed to suit the environment, and everywhere one can find this adaptation to life lived under difficult circumstances. Animals living on rocky ground tend to develop non-skidding feet as have mountain sheep and the Rocky Mountain goat. The webbed feet of water birds tend to keep their possessors from sinking in the mud as well as to aid their swimming. Mammals living on soft substratum have large feet that keep them from floundering, as does the moose, which lives in marshes, and the snowshoe hare, which runs on snow.

Adaptation is one of Nature's favorite methods of problem-solving, and only those who learn Nature's secret of adjustment are prepared to handle life triumphantly.

By adaptation one does not mean compromise of principle. There is a stubborn resistance to undesirable change that

48

is admirable and heroic — the non-compromising attitude of Jesus Christ or Abraham Lincoln. They were unyielding when a principle was at stake. But both were adapters, Christ teaching tolerance and forgiveness, which are ways of adjusting to people, and Lincoln living with his difficult, insulting, overbearing Secretary of War, Edward Stanton, and doing it with cheerfulness and Christian charity. Those who comprise our social environment cannot always be transformed to please us. Often we must accommodate them. If we are big enough, Christ-like enough, we can.

An almost unbelievable case of unyielding stubbornness was revealed by an elderly man some time ago at the funeral of his brother with whom he had shared a tiny one-room cabin not far from Canisteo, New York. While they were still young men they had had a furious quarrel after which they divided their room in half with a chalk line. From that time on neither had crossed the line and neither had spoken a word to the other in their remaining sixty-two years together!

Such people mistake stubbornness for strength of character. They boast of their obstinacy, believing it a sign of personal power. However, much unyielding stubbornness is less a mark of a strong soul than of a weak mind. It is found in generous amounts among the lowest, least intelligent creatures. Ernest Thompson-Seton once told a fable of a stubborn land crab who boasted loudly of his determination and indomitable spirit. "I'm unchangeable," he bragged. "Once I have a purpose in mind nothing can change my course." One spring day the crab left his winter quarters in the hills and began his annual sojourn to the sea. But during the winter a long line of telephone poles had been placed along the land crab's trail. When the crab came to the first pole he paused, thought a moment of turning aside, and then remembered his boasted stubbornness. He would not turn aside. Not one inch! He started up the pole and slipped to the bottom again. But he tried once more, and then again, and again. At last, after an entire day of incredible struggle, he succeeded in climbing up the side of the pole and slid down the other side. Almost exhausted, he started up the second pole. This time, weakened by his efforts on the first pole, he needed many rest periods. But he painfully pushed on. Before the summer was spent the crab's wasted form was found at the bottom of one of the poles, a memorial to foolhardy stubbornness.

Among all the countless species of creatures on this planet, life that is rigidly confined to a fixed pattern is always rated lower in the scale of intelligence. A land crab is lower than a squirrel, being less creatively adaptive. A squirrel is lower than a man, being less flexible, less imaginative, not as capable of adjustment to changes in its environment or of rising imaginatively to emergencies.

Every environment is less than ideal. Every job has its disagreeable aspect. Everyone we meet will have some faults that will not yield to our attempts to reform. Every person has his own kinds of temptations and problems and trials, his own handicaps and sorrows. This is not the way we should like our existence to be, but this is the way life is. If we cannot change the whole universe to suit us, we can be changed to equal the universe.

God's way is not to make life easier, but to make us greater.

12

LIKE THE COMING OF SPRING

APRIL is here.

Now patches of dry, brown grass appear in open fields. Deer eagerly leave the swamps to nibble on tender greening shrubs. Soon the lowlands, ponds, and marshes will ring with choruses of spring peepers singing to the rippling accompaniment of overflowing streams. Warm south winds and soft spring rains will coax apple blossoms from their twigs, violets from forest loam and marsh marigolds from their brookside nests of broad green leaves. Far lighter than a feather's touch, the sun's golden radiance has stroked the earth, and the world awakens, blinks and stirs, flings back its bed clothes, and commences its vigorous sitting-up exercises.

What brings about these changes? Life is reviving here because of something taking place far out in space where the relationship between the earth and sun has been undergoing a change. While for several months the Northern Hemisphere has been turned away from the sun, now the North has begun to incline toward the sun's warm, radiant beneficence. And the sun will do the rest. Until the sun bestows its favors no amount of prying and pushing of seeds will make them grow.

51

No frenzied efforts on our part will bring the warblers from their winter homes or free the frost-bound earth from its chains of ice and wrappings of snow. Something vital is transpiring here because of a change way out there where the influences of sun and earth meet and become cordial. Who would think that the delicate beauty of spring violets and the sweet fragile notes of returning birds had anything to do with the number of degrees in an oblique angle that the earth's surface makes with the ninety-million-mile-distant sun? Yet that is the way it often is with this mysterious universe — something happening here because of another thing happening elsewhere.

The prosperity of farmers near Cairo, Egypt, can be accounted for by plentiful rain high in the mountaintops of the African interior where the Nile River begins. Drought in those mountains means a ruinous lack of water for irrigation of farms thousands of miles away. So it is with life: much of its successful handling depends upon indirect factors. If we want success here at this point, we must begin at another point altogether.

One of life's strangest paradoxes is that many of our most coveted goals are reached not by striving for them, but by aiming at something else altogether. When a person has a serious lung infection, medicine is not forced into the lung. A serum is injected into the arm or hip and must go to the lung indirectly. So in solving life's problems, a cure is often effected through attacking them by a circuitous route, by indirection.

Some people go about life constantly frustrated because their aggressive assaults on life's problems do not yield expected results. They attempt by back-slapping, flattery, and busy-bodied attentiveness to make friends of their acquaintances, and when they have received a back-slapping, flattering, attentive response they believe they have succeeded. But they are soon disillusioned, and find that the reaction will not bear the tests of friendship. A slight misunderstanding, a fervent difference of opinion, and the relationship is broken. A real friendship is seldom formed by aggressively attempting to make a friend out of any acquaintance. Friendship is a by-product of trust, reverence, similar interests, a common standard of values and shared enthusiasms and contentments. When these conditions are fulfilled, friendship arrives unsought.

You have had the experience of trying to remember an elusive name that persisted in escaping you. "Just a minute," you said; "I'll have it in just a minute!" But nothing you could do would force that name from its hiding place somewhere far back in the corridors of memory. So you gave up. Then, hours later, when you were planting a garden, or fishing, or preparing a meal, the lost name came creeping from concealment and identified itself. Often memory is like a shy child — if you go after it aggressively, demanding that it come to you, it flees; but if you sit back quietly, waiting, busying yourself with other interests, it approaches you and tugs at your sleeve, seeking attention.

One of the most noticeable differences among morally good people is found in the presence or absence of radiance. Some are morally good but unattractively so, showing signs of strenuous, pained effort to be decent, bearing the marks of strain on their faces like an amateur soprano reaching for an impossibly high note. Others are radiantly good, with the happy grace of a mother effortlessly singing hymns of joy as she busies herself with kitchen chores.

The secret of wholesome, upright living is not found in merely wanting to be good and seeking goodness with a dogged determination. Effort is necessary, but effort alone is not enough. We do not ennoble our lives by straining to be good. We become better people by indirection, by a conscientious self-examination and repentance for our failures, by fighting difficulties and overcoming trouble and temptation, by imagining ourselves in another person's place and treating him as we should wish to be treated, by seeking to serve world need, by becoming involved in transforming fellowship with people of contagious good spirit, by frequent meditations upon

life's highest and noblest values, and especially by a sustained companionship with God. Aim directly at goodness and you will either be frustrated or become obnoxiously sickening with false piety. Attractive goodness comes to us indirectly.

We all want happiness, but many a person is missing his goal because he is aggressively seeking it. I have known many happy people and countless unhappy ones, and I have been amazed that the miserable people never seem to learn from the happy ones that happiness cannot be had by seeking it. Happiness escapes our intent pursuit, but makes its appearance when we are looking for other things we regard more important. We pursue a mighty purpose and find happiness along the way; or we engage our attention and skill, our time and energy in a worthwhile task, like building a boat, growing roses, painting a picture, educating a child, and happiness joins us, uninvited. We attempt to fill our minds with the most interesting, inspiring, worthwhile thoughts, and happiness slips in with the rest, almost unnoticed. Or we try to make others happy, and while pouring the perfume of pleasure on others we accidentally spill some on ourselves.

Growth in friendships, goodness and happiness, like all growth of spirit, is like the coming of spring. It cannot be had by frenzied effort. It comes when the conditions are met, when we turn thoughtfully and reverently toward the bright radiance of the things that matter most, and toward the light of God.

13

THE GREAT HUNGER

WHILE driving into Hidden Brook a few evenings ago we were treated to a sight that for us was most unusual — a large white-tailed doe lying near the trail and watching us with casual interest. Not until I opened the car door and started in her direction did she leap to her feet and bound away through the grove of budding birches. On very rare occasions we have noticed deer resting in adjoining meadows and fields as we have approached our gate, but usually when we see them the deer are running, or at least walking, on their way to satisfy one of their great hungers. It may be the tissues' demand for energy-giving fuel which will be appeased with maple browsings at the woods' edge. Or it might be a deep-seated, pressing yearning for water, and when the day is spent and darkness shrouds the North, the fretful urgency will be quieted at a peaceful pool where the brook lingers, dawdling briefly on its way to nearby Lake Charlevoix. Or the body's aching for rest will be supplied in the cool, comforting shade of yonder lacy cedar tree. Nearly always the graceful animals are going somewhere, on some errand of satisfaction of a bodily need.

Human nature has this in common with all our kindred of the wild: we are creatures of restless urgencies and gnawing hungers, and when we see people active it is usually when they are satisfying one of life's basic needs. They are at their place of employment earning the wherewithal to purchase food and shelter, or they are found at play seeking relaxation and rest, or they are at home with mate and family fulfilling an inner craving for fulfillment and perpetuation of their kind and seeking the security of being among those who care.

The evils men do reveal their warped ways of attempting to gratify deep desire and end an inner famine. And when evil fastens upon a person he will use any situation to tame the inward urges. Hatred is an example. Hatred is one of life's most perverted, insistent and greedy cravings once it gets a grip on a person. Dr. Walter Bowie has pointed out that hatred is like alcoholism. When a man is controlled by alcohol he will drink anything, not just whiskey or gin. If these are not available wood alcohol will do. Compulsive hatred is like that. Once it seizes a man, he is bound to hate, and not only the things that are hate-worthy, such as disease, cruelty, abject poverty or war. When these are temporarily out of stock, or out of mind, he finds something else to hate. It may be Jews or Germans, Negroes or Mongolians, Catholics or Protestants, Republicans or Democrats. Hatred is a thirst that consumes whatever is near at hand.

Faultfinding is another evidence of perverted appetite. The chronic criticizers do not need devils and wretches to flay and reprove. Anyone will do. A member of a certain church in a Michigan city (thank Heaven, not my own!) has been opposed to every pastor she has had in the past twenty-five years. One preached too loudly. Another was so homely she couldn't thoroughly enjoy his preaching. The next one joked too much, and the following was a hypocrite, so she thought. Now she has one of the finest pastors in the state, a man who serves on many of his denomination's boards and committees. These involve many meetings each year which he must attend. "Why doesn't he stay at home where he belongs?" she asks. Each time she has become acquainted with her minister she has found some fault and has pled for a change, but when the change has come she hasn't liked that either. So far the big change has not occurred — a change in herself. Most churches have one or two of these habitual faultfinders. The preacher speaks too long so that people get restless, or so briefly that he must not have prepared well, and "it was hardly worth coming to hear." He makes too many pastoral calls so that he does not spend enough time studying, or he spends too much time studying and therefore doesn't call enough. He is not enough interested in the young people, or he spends too much time with the young people and pays no attention to the older folks. He is too progressive, always starting something new and keeping things in an uproar, or he's an old fogy and has no new ideas. He is too strict or too lenient, too dogmatic or "he has no convictions."

57

He calls too many committee meetings so that "you never have a night at home," or he runs a "one-man show" and doesn't know how to delegate authority. I have been singularly fortunate. In well over twenty years of public ministry I have never run into a nest of these habitual faultfinders, but I have a profound pity for some of my fellow ministers and their congregations who are afflicted with them.

Faultiness can be detected in all human nature, just as alcohol can be found in some form or other in nearly every town and village, but the habitual faultfinder, like the alcoholic, possesses a compulsion for seeking it out, in husband or wife, in children and neighbor, in club president or community leader or fellow church member, in employer and employee. Once he has found the fault, he seizes upon it, tastes of it with wild-eyed fervor, swallows it in great gulps and gets spiritually sick on it so that he can't see straight or walk uprightly.

Alcoholism has two components — the presence of alcohol in the world, making it available, and the alcoholic's psychological need of liquor either to help him escape from the world or to make him feel temporarily adequate to the world's demands. Just so, faultfinding is compounded of two factors — the fact that everyone is faulty at some point or another and the faultfinder's inner need to criticize (to lower others so that he can feel higher, to find sin in others so that he can feel more righteous, or to develop a feeling of power because he knows that by the strategic use of a few choice words he can hurt, maim, or destroy another's pride or reputation). Faultfinding is one of the world's perverted hungers.

Too many imperfect people are demanding perfect homes and blaming husbands, wives, children, and parents for not living up to their expectations. They would agree with the common sense reasoning that to be human means to make mistakes and to have faults, but in practice they don't want those near them to make any particular blunders. Theoretically they can be imperfect, but in practice they must have reached perfection since whatever fault a husband, wife, or child possesses is precisely the one that cannot be tolerated.

So with daily labor. Any work looks good but the work you are doing. Any town is attractive but the town you live in. Any neighbors could be enjoyed but the neighbors you have. Any woman or man would be better than the one you married. We may seldom give a thought to improving ourselves as workers rather than changing jobs, becoming better citizens rather than moving to another town, being better neighbors or mates rather than insisting they change. One reason for Hollywood-type serial marriage in America is that too many are *looking* for the right mate and too few are trying to *be* the right mate. The kind of faultfinding that is productive of the most good is dissatisfaction with oneself.

The best people as well as the worst are driven by deep hungers, and whenever you see them they are apt to be seeking satisfaction for their intense urges. Some desire to identify themselves with the world's hurt and downtrodden. Walt Whitman, who nursed wounded soldiers back to health and comforted the dying during the Civil War, once said: "I do not ask the wounded person how he feels. I myself become the wounded person." That is compassion of the highest order, arising from a craving of the holiest kind.

Alexander Pope was one of the most hideously deformed men of all Great Britain, and one of its best poets. We owe much to his search for aesthetic beauty through poetic expression and his hungry ambition to be the best poet possible. He once said to himself, "If my person is crooked, my verses shall be straight." And they were.

There is a glory in doing well whatever you are doing, in doing it better than you ever have done before. And there's a grandeur in being better than you were the year or day before. We want the best mates, the best children, the best friends, teachers, ministers and civic leaders. But more important is the desire to be the best kind of a marriage partner, the best sort of a parent, friend, scholar, churchman and citizen.

The best hunger is the craving to become the best we can be.

59

14

TEMPESTUOUS WEATHER AND TURBULENT PEOPLE

WHEN I arose at daybreak this March morning, the earth was freshly spread with a new whiteness. Large, soft flakes were still falling. Then, within moments, the sky changed its mood and began to weep copious tears that splashed against my study windowpane, driven by a low wind off Lake Charlevoix. Again the temperamental weather changed. Giant, fleecy flakes fell once more, soundlessly, white on white. Suddenly all was still. No more snow. No more rain. No wind. Nature lay waiting, quiet, a bit apprehensive. What next? A blizzard? Driving sleet? Pouring rain? A burst of sunshine?

March, the month of contradictions, is here. There will be days of quick, unexpected wintry storms and blossoming crocuses; days of mournful, howling winds and cheerful robin's song; days of sudden cold and surprising warmth; days when skies are alternately a threatening smoky gray and then, again, vivid blue and smiling. Streams will be ice-bound and then leaping and laughing. Broken limbs in our woods tell the history of last winter's blizzards, and the faint lavender on the birches prophesies verdant leafy canopies shading forest trails.

In the month of March, Nature is tumultuous. She cannot make up her mind. One moment she craves springtime; the next she wants another taste of winter. She is vacillating, indecisive. We shall have real spring when the tumult ceases and beauty sprouts and thrives everywhere, when Nature finally says, "Let's have spring," and means it, sticking to her decision. Then the warm sun will snip the bonds of ice that bind our lakes, ponds and streams and free the brown earth from its white wrappings. Ruffed grouse, now hard pressed for food, will feast sumptuously on plentiful green leaves and succulent buds. Those

60

deer that have miraculously survived this winter of deep snows, biting cold, and scarce browsing will dine on choice delicacies of maple, witchhazel, blackberry, and willow shoots and sweet-fern. Tulips will ignite gardens and yards with flames of red and yellow, and beds of marsh marigolds will grow along our brook. Choirs of robins, thrushes, tanagers, ovenbirds and warblers will sing from their lofts in every Northland forest. From ponds and marshes myriad frogs will chorus their elfin music, chanting a traditional tune.

When Nature puts an end to her fickle vacillations, spring can come.

Much tumultuous living is like turbulent March weather: it is due to indecision. When a high-school senior cannot make up his mind whether to go to college, when a college student wavers interminably concerning choice of a profession, when a marriage partner vacillates between faithfulness to marriage vows on the one hand and promiscuity on the other, when a parent is sometimes too strict with his children and at other times carelessly lax and weak, when a person sings hymns and offers prayers like a saint on Sunday but acts like the devil during the week, there is trouble. Such people have not made up their minds; however, they cannot avoid making up their lives. They will go on living and acting one way or another just as throughout March we are bound to have some sort of weather. But the inner weather of a person's life will be stormy and unsettled until he learns to make decisions.

In a significant sense indecision is itself decisive. By "doing nothing" we always do something, and perhaps life's most serious decisions are made when we decide to do nothing at all, at least for the present. Probably no one ever determined, "I will be ignorant." But many a person has postponed a decision on what to read or when to read until he found himself embarrassingly ignorant on the important issues of his time. Few people have ever declared, "I want my child to grow up without any religion whatsoever and to live out his life without firm religious convictions or practices." But many a parent has encouraged a child to live in an atmosphere of suspended decision until the youngster's character was formed and his habits of feeling and thinking were established. This is usually done with the excuse, "Religion is too important a matter to decide for one's children. When they are old enough, they can make up their own minds." But the argument is fallacious. Education is important, too, but we do not allow our children to decide if they will go to school, or when, or on what days of the week. Eating is important too, but we plan their meals; and when, at the age of a few months, they attempt to swallow pins and

needles, tacks and screws, dog hair and dirt, we do not let them make "their own decisions." When at ten years of age they prefer ice-cream sodas for their entire diet, we do not allow them "to make up their own minds." The more important a matter is, the more imperative it is that our children be given some direction and be taught to make proper early decisions. Children are gardenlike growing-places. We are foolish to "let them decide" important matters without careful guidance. Gardens that are not sown with seed, not prejudiced toward fruitfulness or flowers but allowed to "make their own decisions," grow weeds. So with children. Parents' indecision determines that weedlike ideas and moral standards will spring up in the lives of their youngsters.

If we are bound to live one way or another, and even our indecision determines our way of life for us, are there guides to help us make good choices? There are. Here, in abbreviated form, are three principles for settling our spiritual weather, so that turbulent March can be followed by some springtime of the soul.

(1) Our best decisions are made in harmony with our long-range purposes rather than in conformity to our momentary whims and urges. The courting teen-ager will do well to govern his decisions concerning emotional involvement and "petting" in harmony with the kind of mate he wants to find and in accord with the kind of mate he wants to be — guiltless, with nothing to hide and no unpleasant memories to mar his most sacred moments. He asks himself how this conduct will affect what he will later want to do and be. So with everyone of every age, concerning every issue: we need to ask ourselves the traveler's question: "Will this attractive side-road take me to my destination?" If it will not, it is foolish to take that road.

(2) Our best decisions are made on the basis of our lasting responsibilities rather than our transient moods. Every life would be stormy and unsettled if it were governed by fluctuating feeling. But duties are steadier and more dependable. We sometimes feel loving and sometimes bitter, but treating others with mercy and tenderness is a responsibility that is not here today and gone tomorrow. Many a man whose eyes never got married when the rest of him did has been true to his vows because his lasting duty was more important to him than his wavering attention. The people who stabilize the world are those who can be counted upon to pay their dues, do their work, fulfill their promises, attend worship, and support worthy causes regardless of how they feel at the moment.

(3) The simplest and clearest principle I know for making a decision is a very old one, an effective one, used by some people for two thousand years: "What would Jesus do if He were in my place?" And the rule is still as good as new, having suffered little wear.

There are other guides to good conduct, sufficient to make a book or a library, but these are enough to bring a degree of spring out of Marchlike turbulence. Try them and see.

15

THE QUIET-SPIRITED

WHERE the amber waters of our woodland stream run deepest they are most quiet. Where the brook is shallowest, it babbles.

People, too, are generally quietest where they are deepest, and noisiest where they are shallowest.

A lady complained to me some days ago about the treatment she received in a certain dress shop in another city. It wasn't that she was intentionally abused or treated with indifference. Quite to the contrary, she was overwhelmed with frantic attention and swarmed over by clerks who called her

"Honey," "Deary," and "Darling" and constantly fawned over and flattered her. And all of this frenzied attention was given by utter strangers. What offended the customer was the superficiality of the saleswomen. They were babblers. They were using terms of endearment to make a commercial transaction, using words of love superficially. What distinctive words of affection would they have left to use on those most dear to them, their sweethearts, husbands, or their children? Real affection is seldom rash or gushy, nor does it hasten toward some desired reward like a sale. Affection is a deep and quiet pool of appreciation, care, respect, and desire for another's happiness and ultimate welfare and it clamors for nothing in return.

Sentimentality babbles, running in noisy turbulence over shallow souls. We see and hear it where people easily become misty-eyed over the plight of their fellow men without ever performing a generous, loving deed to help them. But genuine goodwill is found in quiet, kindly, thoughtful behavior and it lies action-deep.

When anyone attempts to impress you with his education and culture by the use of long words and affected accent, you can be certain he is not convinced that his education is thorough or his culture deep. Ostentation is a proof of a shallow mind and impoverished soul. One office manager had to let a new stenographer go. He explained his action, saying, "It is too bad. She had a lot of polish, but it was all on her nails." Sometimes intellectual polish is just as superficial; it's all in appearances. A showy vocabulary may serve to disguise meagerness of thought. A large vocabulary is good if it is not showy, noisy, ostentatious; if the big vocabulary is used for carrying big ideas. Nonsense babbles. Wisdom runs in quiet pools.

Beware of the person who boasts of his virtue, his humility, his faithfulness, his sincerity. When someone frequently emphasizes, "Now I'm sincere about this," we naturally wonder why he needs to make the claim. Why the distinction — "sincere about *this?*" Are there things he is *insincere* about, and why? Real virtue does not need to be declared; it will announce its own presence in its own quietly convincing way. Ralph Waldo Emerson once said of a braggart, "The louder he talked of his honesty, the faster we counted our spoons." Of course! A loud and boastful honesty is certain to be shallow and cannot be trusted. Profound honesty needs make no ringing claims. Like a pool in the forest, it can afford to await discovery. It's in no hurry. It's not going dry.

The noisy things of earth are the little things, like the cicada — those raucous locusts that sing on hot July afternoons — and the brook babbling over boulders. The silent things of the universe are deep, like pools and ocean abysses, big like distant mountains, vast like the Milky Way.

Some of us might stand more chance of greatness if we practiced more hours of silence. As a prophet of long ago once said, "In returning and rest shall ye be saved; in quietness and in confidence shall be your strength."

16

WHAT A DIFFERENCE

SCIENCE cannot be understood in terms of the subject matter studied; instead science is differentiated by *how* the study is made. While we sometimes think of science as being the study of birds or of rocks, of plants or of man, upon further thought we see that others besides scientists investigate these subjects, and attitudes other than that of scientific analysis are taken toward them. Ornithologists study birds; geologists apply their knowledge to rocks; astronomers measure the magnitude of the stars; botanists consider the structures, functions and ecology of plants; and anthropologists, sociologists, physiologists, chemists, and psychologists investigate the history, social life, and physical and mental make-up of man.

But all of these matters are also effectively approached by others who have no training and little interest in science; the approach is made by different routes and with different appreciations.

The scientist specializing in bird life, who dissects a bird in the laboratory and examines its music-producing instruments, and the bird-watcher who stands by in wonder while the green cathedral of a wood echoes the fragile notes of a song sparrow's notes are attentive to the same object. The professional ornithologist who makes his living in research concerning birds and in lecturing on bird lore can describe a songbird after a fashion. A systematic ornithologist who specializes in classifying our winged wild neighbors defines all songbirds as those birds which have the "syrinx with four or five distinct pairs of intrinsic muscles, inserted at ends of three upper bronchial half-rings and this constituting a highly complex and effective musical apparatus." That is a scientist's special way of describing a bird like the song sparrow. But when Marian, while out for a stroll, hears the frail, sweet music of a song sparrow and upon her return home excitedly reports it to me, she gives a far more poetic account of the bird's song and appearance than does the ornithologist. His description is coldly analytical and heavy with precision. Hers is warm with fascination and feathery light with joy. Both reports are accurate and valuable, but what a difference in how they are made! Both have some understanding of birds, but what a difference there is between precise analysis and joyous watching and listening!

An X-ray photograph furnishes important information about an eighteen-year-old girl, but it makes a poor and uninspiring likeness for her swain to keep on his dresser. A girl's pulse beat may relate significant data about her health, but she is likely to be most upset if her fiancé, because of scientific interests, counts her pulse to test her reactions while he whispers "sweet nothings" in her ear. X-ray photographs, counting pulse beats, and frequent dating are all ways of knowing a girl but what a difference in method!

The best things in life escape our exacting analysis and precise definitions. This is true of song sparrows and birches, of the Grand Canyon and the Niagara Falls, of the sea and the mountains, of man and God. Just now I am thinking it's especially true of a wife. Mr. Webster, in his best-selling little book, *The Dictionary*, has defined a wife as "a woman; an

adult female" and "a woman united to a man in lawful wedlock."
That is fine and accurate, I suppose. But it leaves too much
unsaid. In fact, *anything* that is said will still leave a great deal
unsaid. But I suppose the writer of a dictionary, like the writer

of a bird book, must approach the word "wife" from the viewpoint of his own experience. If his chief work and main interest is in finding a universally acceptable definition, then that is the way "wife" will be described. But if the same compiler of words were to describe "wife" just after she accidentally spilled a bowl of hot pea soup in his lap, the description would be different. (Probably, after such an exasperating accident the lexicographer would not need to be asked for a description; a most colorful description would be promptly volunteered!)

My own definitions would be these: A wife is that person whose face is the most important in every crowd; she is the one to whom a man must sometimes go to rest from being his best; a wife is that person who not only makes a home for her family, but accommodates in her being ideals of beauty, loyalty, quiet courage, self-sacrifice, gentleness and poise — ideals that are homeless sojourners on the earth until some hospitable soul gives them a place to settle down. A wife is that lovely creature who makes a man want to run the last few steps homeward. Some definitions and descriptions are not in the dictionary, or in sociological studies of marriage and family, nor can they be found in the fine print of thick law books. They arise from the experience and well up from the heart of a most fortunate and grateful husband.

A certain artist always kept a number of beautiful gems near his easel, an emerald, a sapphire and a ruby. When he was asked the reason for these gems in his studio he replied that it is difficult to keep one's colors true. Sometimes they fade or are dulled by faulty mixture. Or an artist's eye can become jaded by too much daily dealing with man-made color. So he kept his eye for color true by referring to original colors that could not fade.

The best definition of color is not in a dictionary or on a chart but in a gem. The best way to know the Grand Canyon is not through a postcard picture but by going there. A bird book can describe a song sparrow's happy carolling, but the best written analysis is a poor substitute for hearing its bubbling joy. Goodness is a religious and philosphical conception upon which heavy tomes have been written, but it's far better to see the genuine article sparkling in a radiant person. I know. I married such a one.

17

A LAKESIDE PRAYER

Lord of the great waters
That ceaselessly flow beneath the vaulted sky,
Hear my lakeside prayer.
Grant me the poise of all floating things —
Waterfowl, water lilies,
Slender canoe and slim sailing ship —
That ride high and trustful
Over great depths,
Sustained by the mercy of the waves.

Lord of the timeless waters
That were here before man was here,
That will remain when man is gone,
Grant me unhurried calm.
Let not the busy beating of the seconds

71

Quicken the tempo of my living
So that I become more of a clock
Than a man.
Let no awareness of swiftly passing moments
Make me forgetful of everlasting things
And the Everlasting One.

Lord of the welcoming waters
That are cordial to inflowing stream,
To ship and swimmer,
And that make room for countless fishes
And other dwellers of the deep,
Make me a welcoming spirit,
With abundant room in my soul
For the cares and griefs,
The enthusiasms and joys,
Of all Thy children,
Knowing that, like the lake lying before me,
The more good things I receive unto myself
The higher I shall rise.

Lord of the pardoning waters,
Grant unto me a forgiveness that forgets a wound
Wrought by friend or foe
As the great waters are cut by a keel,
Ruffled by a breeze,
And buffeted by storm,
But in mere moments resume their tranquillity
As if keels and breezes and storms
Had always been kind.

Lord of the reflecting waters
That repeat the hues of heaven
Upon their bosom —
The azure blue of fair days,
The somber gray of clouds,
The radiant glory of sunsets,
The silver sheen of moon and stars —
Make me reflective, too,
Mirroring in all my days
The magnificence of a Higher Will

72

And a greater glory
Than belongs to man.
Amen.

18

WHEN SEEN IN A CERTAIN LIGHT

THIS has been an unusually bright and beautiful late-autumn day. From the clear arch of the sky falls a shimmering light that bathes forest and field with an unaccustomed splendor. Against a pale blue background of sky, leafless trees are starkly silhouetted. Where a few days ago snow lay thick upon the pasture, the long grasses can now be seen, sharply articulated. Every passing animal and every bird on the wing looks like a different creature from what it does on dull, gray, overcast days. Now all things seem silvered with a soft sheen. Never before have I seen the North look like this on an early December day — never quite so miraculously gleaming, with the air fairly singing with light and all things of earth and. heaven touched with a gleaming glory. This is a different December day.

Light seems delicate and unsubstantial. It is brittle and fragile, being easily broken by falling on a twig, or shattered into countless sparkling fragments by lighting on a pond's dancing surface. Yet this transparent, fragile stuff of nature is used by the Creator to accomplish all manner of purposes. Light is a weaver of shadows, a builder of rainbow arches. Light is the power that runs the food factories of living plants, enabling green vegetation to combine carbon dioxide, water, and minerals to make apples, melons, tubers and nuts.

An increasing amount of light in the day triggers the alarm that awakens sleeping seed and bulbs and times the flowering of all plants. Such seasonal events as the migrating of birds, the changing color of plumage in male scarlet tanagers and bob-o-links, the dramatic transformation from brown to white of the weasel and the varying hare depend upon the length of day and the amount of light in the sky. Radiation of solar light is in some way linked with the welfare of all living things of earth.

But most obvious of all, light is the conveyor of images from the outer world to the seeing centers of the brain. Eyes would be useless without light. All an eye can do is to focus whatever light reaches it on the screenlike retina which lines the inside of the eyeball and leave there an image to be interpreted by the brain. But whether there will be any image at all to be interpreted by the brain of man or beast depends upon light.

The amount and quality of light, as well as the condition of an observer's eye, determines how well we see. The dimmer the light the more things look alike. In bright, clear illumination and at close range you can distinguish between your two neighbors who are of the same size and are dressed in similar fashion, but in semi-darkness you cannot be certain which of them approaches you. Light clarifies differences, sharpens perception and deepens insight.

There are people who lead us into light like that of a bright clear autumn day. They show us where we should stand if we want to see more clearly and understand more profoundly. This is one of the many things the Master has done for us — He has shown us human nature in a new light.

Like a jeweler displaying a choice pearl or diamond to a friend, Christ held human nature in the light of God's love and turned it about carefully, tenderly, and described its meaning until those who watched and heard could hardly believe they had ever seen a human being before. He did this with Zaccheus, with Mary Magdalene, and with a little child, and made such seemingly insignificant people memorable. Never again could they be overlooked as commonplace once Christ had held them to the light.

We all know some people who are Christlike in this sense: they illuminate all things. When we are with them we see more clearly, we understand more deeply. Duveen, the authority on oil painting, was such a person. One late afternoon he stood before a picture he had sold to Andrew Mellon. Duveen was enthusiastically describing the magnificence of the work of art to the purchaser when suddenly a beam of radiance from the setting sun stole through the window and showered the picture with a resplendent glow. When Duveen had finished his ardent detailing of the beauty of the painting, Mr. Mellon said reflectively, "Ah, yes. The pictures always look better when you are here."

Can anything better be said of anyone?

How about you? How do things look when you are near? Better?

First Book
REFLECTIONS ON THE NATURE OF THE WORLD AND MAN

Part Three
MAN IN CONFLICT WITH THE WORLD

19

WE ARE MADE FOR STRUGGLE

THIS is a world of struggle. It was not meant for ease. The earth, an insignificant-appearing particle of cosmic dust whirling among giant stars, represents a limited habitation for humankind. Nearly three-fourths of the earth's surface is covered with the waters of seas and lakes. Burning desert sands, inhospitable mountainsides, and forbidding Arctic and Antarctic ice occupy another large fraction so that the habitable zones are greatly reduced. Moreover, even when man finds a fair climate and good soil, his days are troubled by droughts and floods, inclement weather, pestiferous insects, all manner of diseases and accidents. Then, to these man adds his own brands of strife between nations, races, political parties and city gangs, between rivals for community esteem and coveted positions of honor.

Much effort is invested in making the earth habitable, in decreasing the frictions among men and providing an easier way of life. Look at our inventions. See the long list of gadgets that pour from our factories and notice how many are intended to replace muscle with machine and effort with ingenious equipment. Much of the scientific genius of modern man is employed in freeing man of work and effort, discomfort and pain

and fear. One of the chief goals of man seems to be to eliminate struggle.

Yet struggle is a built-in feature of the world and of man, and if our chief endeavor becomes that of making life easier rather than nobler, we shall but succeed in making our characters weaker and set them in disharmony with the nature of the universe. We are made for a contest with opposing forces, and we need it as surely as the herring gulls drifting past our windows require the resistance of the air in which to fly and as certainly as bass in Lake Charlevoix need the resistance of the water against which they push when they swim.

Morality requires a resisting medium. Without temptation there can be no virtue. Politeness, which is attention to another's interests and needs, represents a victory over our resisting self-interest. Giving our worldly goods to a needy cause or person indicates triumph over the human tendency to hoard our goods. Self-surrender to a great cause denotes conquest of our opposing lust for freedom from discipline and restraint. If character is "the sum of all that we have struggled against," we shall always need trouble in our world if we are to have any real virtue. There can be heroic greatness only where obstacles are equally great, for what is Samson without Philistines opposing him, or David without his Goliath, or George Washington without his Revolution, or Lincoln without his struggle against Civil War? What is a saint without a temptation to sin? What is Christ without His Gethsemane and His Cross?

Eliminate struggle and you exhaust life of its vitality and much of its meaning.

One reason for our twentieth-century veneration of athletes is that we have attempted to strip life of its risks, and now we find we must put the dangers back where we found them — at the heart of existence. Either we do so by direct involvement, such as in thrill rides on roller coasters, or in gambling or speeding on highways, or we do so vicariously by letting another face the danger and then identifying ourselves with him. If life is not hard enough to challenge our courage or rugged enough to test our hardihood, we devise sports that supply the deficiency — football and boxing, tightrope walking and mountain climbing, diving from high boards into deep water, jumping hurdles, and all the rest.

We complain about the uncertainty of life in this day of high speed on the highways and lament the toll of dead and maimed taken by traffic accidents. But, as if traffic had become too tame for us, men race automobiles at perilous speeds on Memorial Day at the Indianapolis Speedway with an awareness that someone is likely to be killed or injured. And thousands pay to witness the hazardous race, many considering the event a failure if there is no grim accident resulting in a spectacular death. Human nature requires some satisfying dangers. Either we seek a challenge and meet a test or we identify ourselves with someone else who is doing so. He becomes ours, "my hero," — and we feel victorious when he wins or grieve when he loses. We are made for a struggle.

Parents need to recognize that this struggle-principle is deeply imbedded in our offspring. We hurt our children beyond measure when we rob them of life's challenges by giving them too much so-called security. In the past one hundred years we have moved away from the farm and into the city, away from "chores" that occupied a youngster's attention and time and tested his muscles and ingenuity. J. Edgar Hoover, an authority on juvenile crime, recently cited

youth's need for interesting things to do when he quoted one youngster as saying, "Just remember it isn't the urge to deliberately do something *bad* that leads a boy or girl into crime. It's the urge to do *something*." We maim the souls of the young when we deny them tasks to perform in the home and the yard. We cripple their spirits when we provide them with excessive protection from life's rigors. We want our children to be courageous, but we attempt to remove from them the testings on which courage is exercised and grows. We want our children to be wise, but we attempt to manage every aspect of their lives so that they make no mistakes, forgetful that it is from the proper management of mistakes that wisdom grows. By removing stimulation and challenge from the young we frustrate their growth.

One chief fault with the church's present appeal to the world is that church leadership is so frequently unconscious of the human need for challenge. The appeal is too often to softness, and the church receives a soft and unenthusiastic answer. How foolish in an age when people are seeking excitement to present an unexciting religion! How stupid, when the world aches for the tension of stock-car races, a tied score in a baseball game, or a rugged duel between champion-caliber football teams, for the church to advertise its central message as "How to Get Rid of All Tensions" and "How to Relax"! It is small wonder that some people regard the churches as secondary bedrooms where they can supplement Saturday night's sleep! The Early Church was no sedative, but a stimulant producing men that turned the world upside down. The function of religion is not to secure for man the easiest kind of life, but the highest and fullest; not to give us easier burdens, but stronger souls.

There are wrongs in our world that should be righted. There are great deeds to be done, high ideals and values that should be realized. Within us there are capacities for zeal, enthusiasm, and fervor that will be spent on either the best or the worst, but one way or the other, they are certain to be spent. We have energies that must be released and they will be expressed in some kind of activity, for either good or evil. We are filled with emotions that are meant to accomplish something, and they will be either well-directed or misdirected. We are made for response. Here are a few struggles worth our while:

(1) To be uncompromising concerning our moral principles in these times when individualism is widely discountenanced
and compromise has become a religion;

(2) To avoid excessive busyness with little things so that
we might have time for big things (for example, to avoid
reading trivia so that we might read great literature and to
avoid small talk so that we might converse on mighty themes);

(3) To keep some goals just beyond our present reach
rather than within easy grasp, like loving those who hate us
rather than only those who love us in return;

(4) To keep our attention on the questions "How good
is it?" "How lovely?" "How enduring?" and "How worthy
of my lasting devotion?" in a generation that tends to ask
only "How much does it cost?"

(5) To beat the person we were yesterday, improving
upon his understanding and patience, his charitableness and
hopefulness and his service to the world;

(6) In spite of all the appearances to the contrary, to keep
in mind, as Jesus did, that people are worth living and dying for.

These goals are only a few of the many worth striving
for, but they are enough to keep you busy the rest of this
week and the rest of your life.

Life is a big fight and a thriller!   Success and a mighty
victory in your struggle!

20

SAVED BY OUR BURDENS

IN recent years there has been more slow, anguished
death among the white-tailed deer of North America
than at any other time since white men reached this continent. Near the end of a long, hard winter, deer die by
the score, little by little losing grip on life. Now, in March,
having suffered one of the severest winters in modern history,
these animal neighbors of ours have nearly used up their

reserves of vitality, and many are surrendering the fight against malnutrition, cold and deep snow. Some weakened deer have been seen to stagger to fresh, emergency supplies of cuttings or baled hay only to sink in death upon the banquet, too exhausted to eat.

The white man is at fault for much of the white-tail's trouble. We have killed off the predators that kept deer at their best. We have slain the wolves, cougars and bobcats that once thinned herds of their weakest and diseased members and held the deer population within bounds. The increasing number of abandoned farms and cut-over forest areas full of young growth for browsings have made for ideal conditions, causing a mushrooming population growth. Unwise over-protective hunting legislation has been passed that is more concerned with sentiment and tradition than with the long-range welfare of the deer herd, with the result that while we sympathetically pass laws that confine deer hunting to a few days in late autumn and restrict the number and kind of deer that can be taken, at the same time we sentence thousands of beautiful animals to the long-drawn-out torment of starvation. In summary, deer were better off when their burdens were heavier.

We all are.

People seek freedom from the burden of work. They save toward the day of retirement and leisure. When retirement comes, they lay their burdens down. Suddenly they are uneasy, at loose ends, and must either find new interests and new problems to solve, and even burdens to bear, or sicken from boredom.

Many a marriage that has survived early financial reverses, the misfortune of losing children, and the hurts of violent disagreements has later floundered. When the children are grown, when a satisfying income is assured, and when the obvious adjustments have been made, life becomes too easy, and boredom sets in. And boredom is more fatal to marriage than any quarrel. Unless exciting, problem-solving projects are found upon which the partners can spend imagination and energy, the permanence of the marriage is threatened. At such a time a burden can be a blessing.

We have striven hard to make the long climb from the dangers of savagery toward a highly developed civilization free of primitive fears. We have left behind us the hazards of the hunt with stones and crude clubs and wars with spears, stone axes and arrows. Now, having discarded those ancient burdens, we feel lost without the problems of the hunt and the risks of war, so modern man hunts for trophies rather than food and fights with weapons that kill thousands at once rather than a single enemy at a time. We plead for more labor-saving devices and more leisure but find little of lasting value to do with our free time and energy so that the new leisure has become one of the vast moral problems of our time with both juveniles and adults. The psychologist Henry C. Link has put it pithily: "All the material advantages of our civilization conspire to make our lives easier and our characters weaker."

Some authorities on the origins of the fine arts believe that painting and singing may have begun among cave dwellers who were handicapped by physical burdens. A cave man crippled in a fight or by a wild beast was no longer an effective hunter. He developed other latent abilities. When the hunters returned home with fantastic stories of their prowess and strength, the cripple interpreted these tales on the walls of the cave, showing in brilliant color the end of the chase when bear and buffalo were dispatched by deftly thrown spears. And the blind man wove the record of pursuit into song, decorating the narrative with spangles of glory unknown to his more fortunate brethren. Without burdens to be borne primitive art forms might never have developed.

Some burdens are necessary if we are to develop our strength, and many a person has discovered his hidden abilities while overcoming his conspicuous difficulties. Frederic Chopin was undersized, his health shattered by a lung disease. Before he was forty the newspapers had several times falsely reported his death. Weak in body, Chopin found his real power in music, and while dying by inches he enriched the world with polonaises, Polish songs, waltzes, ballads, and preludes. Had he been strong of body it is doubtful that the world would have known his name.

Schiller, the German poet, did not find himself until he lost his health at thirty years of age. Before that he was doing fairly well producing dramatic works, but they lacked depth and showed a warped sense of values. Schiller needed

his burden of sickness. When the first shock of declining health subsided, Schiller began his best work and earned the rank of being second only to Goethe in the order of German poets.

Alexander Pope, Sir Walter Scott, Eugene O'Neill, Francis Parkman, Marcel Proust, John Calvin, Florence Nightingale, Clara Barton, William Wilberforce, Robert Louis Stevenson, Beethoven, Pasteur, and innumerable other benefactors of our race were strugglers against vast physical handicaps and disheartening frailties. But they made beauty from life's blemishes. As Alfred Steiglitz, one of the world's outstanding photographers, has said, "All true art, like all love itself, is rooted in heartache."

If we do not have enough heartache of our own to produce beauty in our living, we can always take upon ourselves someone else's misfortunes. But a life without distress is a life without power of good. We need a load of trouble if we are to be at our best.

When the hurricane of 1938 hit New England it stirred up great floodtides that poured down Eastern river beds. White River Junction, Vermont, was particularly affected when the river suddenly rose dangerously. An important railway bridge in that railroad center was threatened by the raging waters and appeared about to be swept away. Seeing the peril, railroad officials ordered heavily loaded freight cars pushed out upon the bridge until the cars filled the double tracks across the structure. The great burden firmly anchored the bridge. The swirling river spent its wrath in vain.

Many a man has been saved by his burdens.

21

BURDENS THAT LIFT

FOR ME

TO

GRUMBLE

ABOUT LIFE'S BURDENS

IS

LIKE A SHIP

COMPLAINING OF THE WEIGHT

OF

ITS SAILS

OR

A BIRD

COMPLAINING OF THE WEIGHT

OF

ITS WINGS.

22

CIRCUMSTANCES ARE REVEALERS

ALONG our favorite stream stand all manner of trees, of several species, of various ages, of differing conditions of health and strength, and here and there across the brook lie other trees that have recently fallen. I suppose if these great plants could reason and talk, the toppled trees would complain of the waters that loosened the soil around their roots and the winds that brought them down. But only a casual glance would reveal that water and winds did not alone vanquish them. Not outward circumstances but inner weakness of root and fiber dropped them in time of testing. When those trees fell, others stood. The same occasion of testing that proved one tree's weakness demonstrated another's strength.

Life's big occasions do not make cowards of us, or heroes. They merely show what we have secretly been all along. The storm that plunges one tree to the earth strengthens another's sinews. The same heat that melts wax hardens clay. What the circumstances of everyday life do to us will ultimately depend upon the character they find within us.

Name the most favorable circumstances that you can think of — fame, power of high position, wealth — and you can recall unwise people who have used such good fortune to their own hurt and to the disadvantage of others. Think of the most adverse circumstances possible — humiliation, powerful moral temptation, ill health, poverty — and there are some people who have used these circumstances to their own advantage and for the world's good.

In the worst and the best villages and cities you will find both good and bad characters. In the least desirable and most fortunate financial situations you can discover people who are inwardly poor and others who are spiritually rich. In the most backward schools and in the most advanced and stimulating educational institutions there can be found both laggards and fine scholars.

Situations, favorable and unfavorable, reveal what we are.

23

LIGHT AND SHADOW

NEARLY anywhere you look in nature you see patterns of light and shadow. On a bright day the tonal contrasts are strong between a gleam of glancing sunlight on the trunk of a cedar and the coarse, intense black of shadows brooding beneath the foliage. Between the polished silver of a Northern stream glimmering in the sunshine and the deep, rippling darkness cast by a drinking deer, there's a world of tonal difference that is one of nature's visual delights.

On a moonlit night the soft, silent radiance of the sun's pale offspring drifts across the earth, stretching a network of soft light and softer shadow and arranging the dim tones of night in vague imitation of the brighter patterns of day. At night Nature does not paint pictures with light, but sketches them on a blackboard with blue-violet chalk. The shadows are there, but they are darkness drawn on darkness.

Day or night the earth is a child of light and shadow, and it is the nature of our existence that we must live among the contrasts. We shall see both, experience both; we have no choice about that. But which, light or shadow, will have the focus of our attention and thought and conversation, that is a matter we must decide for ourselves.

When Lord Haldane, the British statesman and philosopher, wrote his autobiography he told of an incident that could be a lesson to all of us. When he was a young man, he was engaged to be married to an extremely beautiful and desirable young woman. For the six weeks of their engagement, he looked forward to a lifetime of happiness with the one he loved. The youth's joy was boundless. But then, without warning or explanation, the girl broke off the engagement, and we are left with the impression that he never saw her again and never knew the reason why she changed toward him. A great many

years later, referring to this baffling disappointment, Lord Haldane made only this simple but revealing comment: "I was not then, nor have I ever been, anything but profoundly grateful to her for that perfect six weeks." No blame, no bitterness, but gratitude! Lord Haldane once enjoyed a beautiful experience, and he would allow no subsequent frustration or disillusionment to spoil its splendor.

We have a reasonable measure of health all through our youth and well into our middle years or old age. Then perhaps we lose it, and the grumbling and complaints begin. Forgetful of all our past pain-free days, ungrateful for all our hours of radiant vitality and abounding strength, we remember only our woes. And the shadows are allowed to creep across the splendor and dim the glory.

A loved one is lost to us for a little while through death. How disposed we are to complain, "Why should God take him away?" when we might just as well ask, "Why should God have given him to us in the first place?" Great bereavement is the reverse side of great mercy, and loss the opposite side of gain. We could experience no sadness at another's death if we had not first known the joy of his companionship. While knowing we shall miss him, should we not also acknowledge how his presence companioned our best hours, and while we sorrow at a dear one's departure, should we forget his glad coming into our days?

All this is no argument for teeth-clenching stoicism, but reason for tempering our disappointments with gratefulness and our heartaches with thanksgiving. Some shining glories have been ours and no later disappointment should be permitted to steal their splendor.

24

SOME THOUGHTS ON PAIN

ONE of the chief limitations of all members of the animal kingdom is that they have many of man's experiences without man's attempts to understand them. Death is one example. Pain is another.

The wily weasel roams our land all year round hunting its prey, and now in ermine garb stalks snowshoe rabbits and white-footed mice. It deals out death without knowing what death is, and finally the weasel dies without knowing it is dying. For life and death, although they are experienced by weasels, rabbits, and mice, are not pondered by them, weighed on some delicate scales of logic, tested for doctrinal orthodoxy, or debated at learned forums. They live but do not try to understand life. They die without wondering about the significance of death.

So with pain. A woman slicing bread cuts her finger and it "hurts" and she is much aware that it pains her. A man pounding a nail hits his thumb and everyone in the room hears the shout of anguish, and hours later at the dinner table they laugh at his clumsiness, and he relates how it happened, shows the discolored appendage, and tells, half ashamed, how much it pains. But part of his problem is in knowing that it hurts, in embellishing the momentary anguish of the hammer blow on his thumb with memory and with concern. A hunting dog, on the other hand, will rip his ears on brambles or barbed wire, yelp with the pain, and then, forgetting all about it, carry a retrieved pheasant to his master, eyes shining with mixed triumph and worship. Pain was felt, but not pondered nor understood. So a weasel can inflict suffering or receive it without knowing its meaning. All animals can, and this is one of their severest limitations: they can have man's experiences without savoring them.

97

Several years ago in the state of Ohio a child was born who did not cry. Air had to be forced into its lungs because the youngster did not make the initial lament that signifies a baby's joining the race of men. As the child grew older, there were signs indicating that it was the victim of a rare condition: it could feel no pain. When she was accidentally pricked with a diaper pin she did not protest. She never cried when she bumped her head or fell or burned her hand. Doctors were consulted and they warned the parents that their daughter was afflicted with a dangerous malady. Feeling no pain, she could contract an infection and be unaware of it until it had spread too far to stop. A growth could begin and progress to an incurable stage without giving any outward sign of its presence.

Ordinarily we think a painless existence would be ideal. But it would be perilous, for pain can be a friendly thing. Like the swinging red light and lowering gate at a railroad crossing when a train is coming, it shouts "Caution!" at us.

But pain is more than a warning to the mind that something is wrong in the body. Pain is a momento of our finiteness, reminding man as it does no other creature that his body is a temporary kind of thing, filled with imperfections and sharing the fate of every living organism. It is perishable. It is a reminder we need. For in our facing up to the brevity of our time here we are apt to make a maximum effort to make our days count. It is because our bodies are here so briefly that we attempt to leave behind us some signs that we were here at all. So we seek to perpetuate the best that we know of goodness, truth, and beauty in our children, who inherit the earth from us. We erect buildings, monuments and statues that have a firmer hold on time than we have. We print words and paint pictures and establish charities that outlast us.

Pain, that flashing memorandum of our temporal finiteness, recalls to us, too, how limited are our opportunities to do good. "I, like all other human beings, have but a short while here," the aches and hurts suggest to us. This also means, "All other human beings, like myself, have only a little while to spend here. We are all in this thing together, all time-limited, all merely passing through this valley. Life is too brief to hate, to be mean, to be small." As Henry Amiel put it, ". . . We have not too much time for gladdening the hearts of those who are traveling the dark way with us. Oh, be swift to love! Make haste to be kind!"

If we will have it so, pain will stimulate the growth of gratitude. We learn to appreciate health through the lack of it. Probably no one ever relishes health until he has experienced illness, no more than one can thoroughly appreciate honesty and truth until he has seen shame and hypocrisy, or be profoundly grateful for freedom until he has been denied it, or savor joy until he has encountered disappointment. The person who boasts he has "never had a sick day" hardly knows what health is because he has never experienced in his own flesh and bones and nerves the anguish of suffering. He is to be pitied. He probably finds it impossible to "enjoy good health," consciously and with exhilaration, for he has never experienced the difference between pain and painlessness.

Pain can make us better people just as well as it can make us worse. It can sweeten as well as embitter us. Or to be more exact, it brings out whatever is already in us. Pain is a revealer. It does for us what cutting does to a diamond in the rough. If there are flaws there, cutting accentuates them. If beauty is there, cutting enhances it. But even a diamond of high quality will remain dim and lusterless until it has been cut many times by an expert. Then the many facets will catch, reflect and glorify the light. It is not only the quality of a diamond or its size that gives it value, but the cuts it receives. The big question then, as Shakespeare said, is this:

"In sickness let me not so much say, am I getting better of my pain, as am I getting better for it?"

One of the most important lessons life has to offer is this: it is not so bad to simply suffer pain. What is worse is to endure pain without making something good of it. It is wasteful to possess it, like a "diamond in the rough" and not to cut and polish and make a gem of it.

25

AGAINST A DARK BACKGROUND

THIS past week the Northland has been treated to an exciting, awesome display of aurora borealis — the northern lights. Many times each year one can see the night sky faintly illumined by soft bands of white, but during the first week of October this year the sometimes lightly tinted blue-black sky above the pines was lavish with streamers of pale green, yellow-green, yellow-orange and gray violet. Long ribbons of light were unfurled from the horizon in an arc circling far to the east and the west. From the earth they were cast toward the zenith, from which they soon rolled earthward, only to be flung again high into the skies.

This nighttime wonder usually lasts for only a few hours, but occasionally it continues for as many as sixty hours on the dark side of the earth, so that it can be seen from a given place on three successive nights. And why only at night? Because, although the northern lights are present in the day sky, their beauty can be seen only against a background of darkness.

We ordinarily think we see better in the daylight than we do at night. But that isn't necessarily so. There are some things that, like the northern lights, must be seen at night or missed altogether. We can study astronomy from a textbook while drenched with brilliant sunshine, but communion with the stars can be enjoyed only when we wait for the dark silences to set them free from their daytime obscurity.

101

If we lose something of value outdoors, we may decide to wait for morning "when we can see better." But there are times when the lost can be found more easily in the dark. When the *Republic* was sinking in 1910, another ship, the *Baltic*, sailed to the supposed location of the troubled vessel but could not find her for the light fog that lay low over the ocean. For hours the search went on as the *Baltic* cautiously poked its way through the fog and whistled mournfully. Then night fell and the passengers on the *Baltic* gave up hope of finding the sinking ship in the darkness. But the blackness of night blessed the search. As darkness deepened, the lights of the *Republic* became visible in the distance. The ship that could not be found in the misty light of afternoon could be seen in the night, and rescue followed.

Most of us tend to be more perceptive, more aware of some things in darkness than in light. Prosperity and success tend to lower upon our existence a haze that obscures life's central questions and its basic answers. We cannot see ourselves as we really are in the light of good fortune. But when a dark calamity descends, unknown facets of character are disclosed. Our weaknesses show up our feeble faith, our anemic courage, our vapid dedication to the Highest. When life is sunny, many spiritual infirmities are hidden from us that only darkness reveals. If the moneyed man's wealth is his only strength he begins to know himself when his money is gone or when he suffers a loss that no amount of money can replace — when health is lost, or when one dearer to him than life dies. If one's chief security is in physical well-being, then self-knowledge is greatly increased by prolonged illness. If public acclaim

is one's basic aim, a- chievement, pride and joy, and if only in that does he find peace of mind, then knowledge of self is enhanced when the public applause sub- sides and dark disfavor falls upon him. When life is radiant with suc- cess or even slightly hazy with moderate prosperity many spiritual infirmities are hidden from us that only darkness reveals.

Moreover, not only our hidden weaknesses but our secret strengths are revealed by darkness. John Milton's blindness was more than a bleak tragedy; it was an adventure of self-discovery and his most sublime poetry emerged from that midnight of the spirit. Beethoven's darksome deafness seemed like the end of his musical creativity; instead, he discovered new dimensions of his genius after the dreadful nightfall. The brightness of Paul's intrepid faith did not shine until after he was severely persecuted and imprisoned. Until it was tested by darkness, Paul did not know how much faith he had. Trouble is a revealer, showing both our weaknesses and our strengths.

In the daylight of success and triumph we may seem self-sufficient, but in the night of trouble we see the importance of others. How revealing is another's nearness when deep sorrow settles over us, how dear every face, how meaningful every handclasp. Mabel Cratty has written, "One of the great accompaniments of all the trouble and sorrow we experience is the sense of being knit into the life of our kind. So much more you must be feeling yourself a part of all whom you meet — a partaker in the loads which suffering humanity carries upon its shoulders." Trouble is a revealer, showing us others of whom we have been too little aware, showing us that we need them and that they need us.

More important, in the darkness we sometimes encounter the God who has been near us all along but unnoticed. Our light-dazzled eyes did not recognize Him. God is near whenever there is unselfish love, but too often we miss God and see only human values in that love. God is present whenever there is beauty, but too frequently we recognize beauty as the product of man's genius or the expression of an impersonal "Nature." God confronts us in goodness; but He is easily overlooked, as virtue is credited to man's heroic striving after perfection. But when a gloomy personal tragedy falls, obliterating for a time all the help human love and goodness and natural beauty can offer, what then? Then many a man finds God near, as did Moses in the desert and Isaiah in Babylon.

Indeed, perhaps this is the hope of our time both for individuals and for the whole of mankind: light is dimming. The once-vaunted belief in inevitable human progress is fading as our very advances threaten to annihilate us, and an eagerness for God intensifies as the gadgets of civilization fail to provide peace and fulfillment. As our bright hopes for the ultimate triumph of man's genius fade and utterly fail, the final victory of God's grace can be seen against the darkness.

Second Book

REFLECTIONS ON LIFE'S VALUES AND ITS DESTINY

Part One

SOME THINGS THAT MATTER

26

THE REAL THING

WALKING is conducive to wondering — especially when one is sauntering through the woods in the snow on a cold and brittle day. A woolly white blanket muffles the sounds of earth, until the world is so quiet that one can almost hear the cold, distant morning star, Venus, squeaking as it turns on its axis. And one is never more all alone with his thoughts then when he trudges along a snow-drifted trail in a Northern woods.

So today, while at the woods' edge, I fell to thinking about the nearness of Christmas, and how it would soon be time to cut our Christmas tree and pull the box of decorations out of storage, and purchase a fresh supply of artificial icicles and imitation snow. And I grinned foolishly at the incongruity of it all. We cut or buy our Christmas trees while evergreens stand all about us in the woods — the real things, not severed from their roots and mutilated. We buy artificial icicles and snow to spread over the limbs and beneath the boughs of our Christmas trees while real icicles hang sparkling from our eaves and real snow blankets the sleeping earth. Aren't we human beings odd creatures, paying money for uprooted and maimed trees and artificial icicles and imitation snow when all we need to do is look about us to see and enjoy the genuine articles?

But that is the way with our race. Human beings are those creatures who will indulge themselves in expensive imitations, when the real thing can be had for a lesser price. Take happiness, for instance. Real happiness is not as costly as its counterfeits. The most miserable people I know are those who have made happiness their chief goal in life and are trying to buy it, and in their eagerness to possess it they purchase many a cheap copy of the genuine object. They pay excessive prices in honor for popularity and in physical and moral health while reaching for pleasure. They spend intemperately on whims and baubles that fail to satisfy their quest. The happiest are those who do not seem to be seeking happiness at all, but have found someone to love, some work they enjoy doing, some causes worth serving, some purposes to live for, some hopes worth treasuring.

Real love may cost us anxiety and suffering (for the things we love most can hurt us most), but even then it is less expensive for our mental and moral health than those imitations that pass for love — flirtations, infatuations and infidelities. They are extravagantly costly in honor, trustworthiness, and peace of mind.

Fake friendship that rests upon gushy flattery is an expensive commodity. It is a little like blackmail — there is no end to the payments that must be made. Miss one installment of praise and the relationship is threatened with catastrophe. But real friendship is far less complicated; it consists of simply being a friend.

Imitation religion is always more costly than the genuine article. Hypocrites pay for their deceit with the constant fear they will be detected, and with the apprehension that the

crises of life will disclose a break in the thin veneer of piety overlaying their pretense. But when one's faith is genuine he can allow it to be examined, tested, and tried with the serene confidence that beneath the surface it is as solid and trustworthy as it appears to be. Life's testing treats faked and genuine religion as fire does paper and precious metal. Fire destroys paper and refines gold. Serious trouble dissolves pretenses and purifies real devotion.

Life's expensive imitations remind one of certain exorbitantly priced toys in the department stores for the elite. The customer pays more for a toy bunny than a real rabbit costs, and a life-size toy horse is priced higher than a flesh-and-blood pony. And the imitations are far less satisfying than the real thing. Bishop Bruce Baxter once told of a man whose young son wanted a horse for Christmas. A horse was the only thing on the boy's Christmas list. The father bought the three-year-old a beautiful picture of a horse, done in vivid colors. But the boy complained, "That isn't a real horse!"

The father then bought the lad a book of horses, showing every type from Indian pony to Arabian racer, hoping that the many pictures would placate the youngster. Still the boy was displeased.

His dad searched the toy stores and found a life-size cardboard horse that could be assembled at home, and he helped the lad put the horse together. Yet the three-year-old was annoyed and discontented, and when his father explained that the gigantic toy was the color of a horse and the size of a horse, the boy plaintively and fretfully answered, "But Daddy, it is not a real horse. It's made of cardboard. I want a horse that's made of horse!"

It may be that one reason we are discontented and fretful in our times is the prevalence of the man-made and the artificial. We need a simple insistence upon reality — horses made of horse, happiness with a content of genuine joy, love made of true love, friendship that is little else but friendship, and religion packed with earnest devotion.

27

NEARLY BLIND, ALMOST DEAF

WE human beings walk about the earth nearly blind, almost deaf, and with other senses greatly dulled. Comparatively speaking, this is so. No known human being can see nearly as well as most birds do. Birds can far more rapidly change the focus of their eyes than can man, seeing both at longer and shorter distances as if they were equipped with built-in microscopes and telescopes. Ornithologists rate the sparrow hawk's vision as eight times better than man's and declare that an owl can see ten times more clearly in dim light than can a human being. An eagle, watched with powerful binoculars, has been known to sight a small fish from a distance of three miles and to plunge directly on it. Besides this telescopic vision of birds, their microsopic abilities enable them to notice and define what is far too small to engage man's attention.

When compared with many of the other creatures of earth, human beings appear to have "a cold in the head and can't smell a thing." Go for a walk with a dog and see how he seems almost oblivious of you and wholly preoccupied with smells that drift through his consciousness. He runs with his nose to the ground, savoring odors of which humans are entirely unaware. This scent tells him a squirrel has recently loped over the trail. Another odor brings the news that a toad sits hidden under yonder fern. The dog's twitching nose investigates trees and stumps and holes in the earth that might be dens, and scouts every vagrant breeze. His olfactory lobes, the smelling patches that pick up scent, if spread out flat would have forty times the area of a man's. This means that a human's smell perception is a trifling thing compared to that of a dog.

Still more wondrous than a dog's smell sensitivity is the scent awareness of some insects. If you hold a big female

111

moth an inch from your nose you will smell nothing. But place
her on the inside of your window screen and she will attract
male moths from all over the countryside. Henri Fabre, ex-

perimenting with peacock moths, proved that a female's scent will draw males from a distance of nearly a mile. And that is not all. A male moth can detect from a great distance by his remarkable sense organs whether or not a female has mated!

Compared to dogs and moths, our capacity to perceive odors and fragrances is a dim, dull thing.

The human sense organs for hearing, too, are weak when compared with those of other creatures. A dog can hear his master's footsteps long before human ears are aware of them. Moreover, among the noises of many shuffling feet the dog can discern his master's own peculiar step. While in flight, bats emit squeaks pitched so high that no human ear can detect them, and use their non-stop squeakings to guide them in their nighttime aerial journeys. The sound waves of the bat's squeaks are echoed back from the objects lying in their path, and bats can judge by the time it takes for an echo to return to them just how far off the obstacles are. Thus they dodge dangers they never see.

During World War II hydrophones were developed for detecting the sounds made by enemy submarines. With these instruments faint distant noises were picked up, amplified and interpreted. Many times sailors operating the hydrophones were alarmed by sounds they thought spelled disaster, only to discover the vibrations were made by noisy schools of fishes communicating with each other through odd grunts and squeaks. It is now believed that certain fishes send through the water vibrations sensed by others of their kind, and that these messages help keep schools of fishes together much as the constant calling of migrating flocks of warblers maintains the unity of the flock. Yet these vibrations cannot be detected by human beings without the aid of instruments.

Robins are thought to detect soft sounds of earthworms crawling through the soil. Virtually sightless moles can hear the tiniest thud of an insect falling in a distant room of their tunnel and rush to the newly discovered meal. The natural world is crammed with sounds beyond our narrow range of perception.

It may be a great mercy that our senses are no sharper than they are. Judged by the high incidence of mental disturbances, human minds seem to be burdened as much as they can stand now with the information gathered by our dull receptors. The clamor of this Age of Noise, assaulting the mind with a confusing blast of automobile horns, ambulance and fire-engine sirens, the din of radio and television, the whine of caterwauling, sentimental songsters singing of lost loves is enough to test our reason. What intolerable trouble would assail us if the aperture of sound awareness were enlarged so that in addition to present noises ultrasonic waves reached our consciousness!

Not long ago students experimenting with sound vibration in a university laboratory placed a boll weevil gnawing on a cotton leaf near a sensitive microphone and then amplified the sound of the weevil's chewing. Soon the amplification reached such dimensions that the racket brought the police from their station several blocks away. Small noises, like an insect's chewing, are carried on the air constantly. The dimness of our hearing spares us the sound.

Radio waves are spread all around us. How fortunate we are that we need special equipment to catch them, convert them into a current variation and thence back into sound waves. If our natural senses were enough to do this work the din ringing in our brains would be beyond endurance. Or again, let us suppose we were born with ready-made television equipment in our heads, as we have eyes, and pictures of far-off performances and events constantly danced in our brains. How we would pray for a moment's respite! Yet those pictures are flashing through the world. But our receptors are weak or non-existent, and we are mercifully spared by nature from the muddle that man-made receivers often bring us.

Mercifully the Creator has exempted us from the extension of senses some of our fellow creatures possess. There is blessing in our deprivation and mercy in our dullness.

The real tragedy of dim human awareness is not found so much in our limited capacities as in our non-employment of such consciousness as we possess. Here lies our real poverty. Our souls are poor not because of what we cannot see or hear, but because of what we could sense but do not. The beauty is here; the goodness and glory are spread all about us, awaiting our perception and enjoyment.

Open the Bible almost anywhere and you will find a sentence beginning, "Behold . . . ." The spiritual leaders of the race have always said, "See! Look! Something vital

114

and exciting is going on. Don't miss it. Behold!" No one can read the New Testament without being impressed with the way Jesus used His eyes. He saw what others missed. He noticed a poor widow casting her mite into an alms box while His disciples were absorbed in the bigness of the temple. He was attentive to little children who were being ignored by other adults. Jesus was aware of lilies growing in the fields, of flocks of sheep grazing on the hillside, of nesting birds in the trees, and of these little events He made unforgettable parables, bidding people, "Behold the lilies! Behold the birds of the air!" Behold! Look at what is going on, and see what it means.

Jesus shared the same environment thousands of others daily experienced. But what a difference in what He saw and how He interpreted it! Everything was more than an object. Everything was a revelation of what God is like and what God is doing in this world.

Well, I'm not through, but I'm quitting. You can apply this principle of using such senses as you already have to add to your own experience as I intend to do with mine. Right now, I'm forsaking the use of this pen to step outside and use my eyes and ears.

Want to come along?

28

NOTICING THE SIZE OF THINGS

LOOKING at life clearly means seeing everything in perspective, noticing the relative sizes of things. The spiritually sightless and morally blind miss seeing what is plain to the perceptive — that in this world of variety everything has its own dimensions, and that we must distinguish between the large and the small.

What a dreary world this would be if our winter scene were composed of snowflakes, stumps, trees, and chickadees

that were all exactly the same size. Snow-flakes have their own dimensions. So do stumps and trees and chickadees. And so does everything else in nature and in life. Good living is based, in part, upon recognition of the relative magnitude of things.

Sir Edward Marshall Hall, an eminent English lawyer, brilliantly planned a victory in a famous court case with the use of perspective. He represented Lord Beaverbrook who was being sued by Lady Terrington. The renowned lady charged that Beaverbrook's newspaper, *The Daily Express*, had libeled her, criticizing the clothes she wore, and she demanded exorbitant damages for the injury she claimed her reputation had suffered.

Sir Edward timed the case so that its close would fall on Armistice Day. Furthermore, he so arranged the presentation of his defense that the two minutes of national silence would interrupt his concluding remarks to the court. When the hour of eleven struck, Sir Edward was delivering an impressive summation of his case. But suddenly he stopped. Everyone arose. All stood with their heads bowed for two minutes, feeling mixed sorrow for the heroic dead and gratitude for their immense sacrifices. Then the silence ended. The great lawyer continued his summation, but quietly now and solemnly.

"Members of the jury," Hall said, "we have just commemorated our greatest national sacrifice. We have all suffered grievous losses from the war." Then pivoting about and facing the plaintiff, he exclaimed, "And now we turn from the painful remembrance of our heroic sacrifices to the trifling grievances of this lady." Lady Terrington's hurt vanity was set in perspective, contrasted with the sufferings of millions of Englishmen, and her wounded pride could not pass the test. She did not win a farthing.

How small our grumblings and complaints seem in contrast to the great woes of the world: the starvation in India, the political oppression of Red China, the perpetual terror in Soviet Russia, the pain in hospitals, the grief precipitated daily by accident and crime!

116

How trivial seem the foolish impulses and absurd whims of the moment when compared to the importance of a high and noble lifetime purpose!

In a lifelong pursuit of education one will meet with a multitude of disappointments, but what do they matter when compared with a deepened understanding of God's world, of other people, and of ourselves?

Temptations may be hard to bear, but what is a moment's indulgence, or a day's foolish pleasure, when compared to a mind free of secret regret, or the fear of being found out, or of shame at having betrayed a trust?

There are abundant irritations in caring for a baby. But how much do they count when compared to the worth of that child and what he may someday become?

The morning's burnt bacon is something of a minor catastrophe at breakfast, but is it really enough to cause one to snap at the children, to criticize one's mate and to embark upon the day with a mind leaking pessimism and filled with discontent?

What a difference would be made in our daily living if we would employ time and attention in noticing the relative size of things!

29

WHAT CAN WE AFFORD?

LOOKING from my study window across the bay I see Charlevoix lying there on yonder shore, a town of nearly three thousand people of all ages, of various colorings, of many heights and girths, of all manner of shades of thinking and faiths. They live in homes that range from hovels to mansions, and they are of a wide range in economic status.

In some yards the passer-by can see shabby little rowboats, recently purchased second hand and now being sanded and readied for painting by the proud owners. Those boats aren't much, but they are the best the owners can afford, and when used for trolling for bass or fishing for perch, they may be enjoyed as much as the biggest, fanciest yacht. At the city docks yachts are beginning to assemble, some small ones with sleeping space for two, others nearly liner size with accommodations for a sizable crew and many guests.

But whether the vessel is a two-place rowboat or a magnificent, seaworthy ship, the enjoyment of the lake this summer will depend not upon the size or cost of the craft but upon the inner appreciations of the people who own and handle them. The poorest owner of the smallest boat on the lake and the richest proprietor of the most splendid ship in the harbor are alike in this: they can both afford the best that the lake region has to offer. The best is within reach of everybody here. Anyone, regardless of the dimensions of his boat or the size of his bank account, can absorb the wholesomeness and beauty spread around him in the Northland if he has developed the inner qualities of curiosity, wonder, reverence, and a desire to merge himself with all the good that lies out there beyond himself.

That is not to say "The best things in life are free." They are not. Beauty is not free. Beauty is about ten percent the

loveliness of a view and ninety per cent the appreciation in the viewer, and appreciation of beauty costs time and attention that we must withdraw from the busy whirl of activities that tend to absorb us. Knowledge is not free, hanging ripe from handy trees to be casually plucked by every passer-by. It lies deep beneath surfaces. Knowledge is an ore that must be mined and smelted with tremendous expenditures of labor. Happiness is not free but elusive and costly. It escapes those who chase after it and comes to those who live for others and sacrifice for great causes. Worthwhile character is not free, but the reward of struggle and self-discipline and the result of lessons learned from failure.

However, the best things, while not free, are within our reach. We all can afford them. We have the wherewithal to buy them if we are willing to pay the price in time, in concentration and appreciation, in digging beneath surfaces, and in sacrifice and struggle.

Then, again, there are some things too expensive for any of us, the poorest and wealthiest alike. When I hear people complaining of the things they cannot afford, I wonder why they don't include the things that cost the most: envy, haughty and self-protective pride, and malice.

One of life's greatest tragedies is that so many people are spiritually bankrupt, harboring feelings that no one can afford, and one of earth's chief glories is that we all can have the best things in life if we are willing to pay the price.

30

A MERE MATTER OF DEGREE

ALTHOUGH we do not often stop to think of it, the terms "life" and "death" do not necessarily represent a clear-cut difference. When is a creature alive? When is it dead? It is easy to say when the creature is a human being or a dog or a chickadee. Our dog Lass bubbles over with life, bounding over these snow-swept acres today as if an excess of energy is burning holes in her veins and must be spent. There is no doubt that she is very much alive, as are the chickadees that twist and dart about our wood's edge, chiming sweet elfin music. And when their time comes to be gathered to the dust, dog and chickadees will all be clearly, unmistakably dead.

But among the simpler animals it is nearly impossible to detect a difference between life and death. Take, for instance, the bear animalcule, the merest morsel of protoplasm. It lives in water, which protects it from rapidly changing temperatures, from harmful ultraviolet rays in sunlight, and from the more mischievous effects of gravity. While water remains around it, the bear animalcule is intensively active, rushing about at breakneck speed, capturing and absorbing its food and performing all the functions of its microscopic existence. But if its water environment evaporates, as it sometimes does, the animalcule dries up too, withering into a tiny particle of cellular dust. To all appearances it is dead.

Days pass — and weeks and months. Then the bit of dustlike substance is picked up by a passing breeze and transported to a nearby pond where it is dropped into the shimmering water. Floating there for hours, its tissue becomes thoroughly soaked. Then slowly, ever so slowly, the bear animalcule begins to move. Moments pass and its movements become more vigorous. Soon it engulfs and consumes a particle of food and resumes all the other functions that are a part of living.

In spite of all its deathlike appearances the animalcule has not actually died but retreated into a much lower degree of living, and then, when the proper conditions are met, the molecular morsel is quickened into a fuller expression of life.

Life is sometimes dormant and then again vibrant, sometimes subtle and again conspicuous, sometimes delicate and again rugged and tough. Animals and people are not only alive, but more or less alive, and the degree to which they are alive is important.

In fact, whenever we investigate life's various experiences with discernment we see that "degree" has high significance. An expression commonly used by many of us is "It's merely

121

a matter of degree." What do we mean by "merely"? Are degrees negligible, trifling matters? A person lightly excuses himself of some moral failure, saying, "We all have our faults. It's merely a matter of degree!" The word "merely" is supposed to signify that the extent of wrongdoing is inconsequential. But it is important. There is a wide gulf of moral difference between the person striving for godliness who slips and falls and arises to march on toward his goal and that other person who, when he stumbles and falls, lies there and wallows contentedly in his sin. Even those who alibi their misdoings on the grounds that morality is a relative matter and sinning is but a matter of degree are false to their own argument, for they dare not carry sinning to an ultimate degree. Do you personally know anyone with easygoing attitudes toward morality who dares to sin wholeheartedly, imaginatively, without any restraints whatsoever, and who sins in every direction and at every opportunity? Such determined sinning would be utterly self-destroying — and soon. The difference between the inadvertent failures of human nature and the determined transgressors of the laws of God and man may superficially appear to be a matter of degree. But it is the difference between clumsily stepping into a pond or drowning in it, the difference between life and death.

Pick at random from life's diversities any number of experiences and see how much degree really matters. Two cars meet in the darkness on a highway. One driver politely dims his headlights. The other leaves on his brights. The one driver, blinded by bright lights, runs into a bridge abutment and is killed. Still, the difference between bright and dim lights is only a matter of degree.

Most of my friends have good vision, a few have "perfect" eyesight, and a very few are nearly blind. The quality of their vision is but a relative matter — a matter of degree — but how consequential to them whether they can see objects clearly in broad daylight, or can only discern shadows moving about in a hazy, unreal world.

A prisoner is free to move about in his six-by-six-foot cell. You are free to move about all over America. As far as physical freedom is concerned you both have some. The degree makes a real difference, doesn't it?

A few days ago a Michigan man was found frozen to death a few paces from his parked car. It was only a matter of degrees of temperature, but how serious a matter to him, his widow, and his children.

Your dearest loved one has a normal body temperature of 98.6 degrees Fahrenheit. When he is ill you watch his temperature closely and anxiously. If it reaches 105 degrees you know he is very sick indeed, and if it should soar as high as 109 and linger there for hours his chances of survival are very slim. Yet it is "just a matter of degrees"!

Nearly everyone on some occasion finds fault with our way of existence here on earth, its hardships, frustrations, and pains. But then, too, there are the faultfinders who make a hobby of complaining. They fuss and fume daily. Faultfinding may be "only a matter of degree," but what a difference a few degrees make!

All of us have some faith in something. The farmer has faith in the value of plowing, sowing, and cultivating. The miner has faith or he would not sink his shaft. The explorer has faith or he would not launch his ship. The devout has faith or he would not whisper his prayer. Of first importance is what we believe in, and of next importance is how much we believe. What one of us does not need a stronger faith in God? Yet "stronger" and "weaker" are but words denoting "a mere matter of degree."

We are placed here on earth to add what we can to the world, not to get all we can from it. How much we add is "merely a matter of degree," but how important a matter it is.

"Life is like a ladder," as Roger Babson put it. "Every step we take is either up or down." And how important it is how far up we go — or how far down.

No one ever became extremely wicked all at once.

Every great and Godlike person has become so gradually —by degrees.

The "mere matter of degree" is one of the most important matters in the world.

31

KNOWLEDGE: NEW AND SECOND HAND

OF all the naturalists America has produced — Audubon, Henry David Thoreau, W. H. Hudson, John Burroughs, and the rest — the wildest of the lot was John Muir. He traveled widely in the nineteenth-century American wilderness, alone, unarmed, unafraid and perfectly at home. He was stimulated by hardships and delighted in hard work. When night overtook him he could find a sheltered spot almost anywhere and lie down to untroubled sleep.

"John of the Mountains" he was called, for he loved the Sierra ranges and doubtlessly knew them more intimately than any man before or after him. But he could have been named "John of the Forests" just as appropriately, for trees were his friends. One of his best-known essays describes his reckless ride in the top of a wildly whipping Douglas fir tree during a violent wind storm near the Yuba River in northern California.

Not only did John Muir travel deep into the wilderness, but the wilderness went deep into him. His sense of honor towered like a virgin pine and his manner was as forthright and unmistakably plain as a mountain peak. He was free as the wind, unbound by convention. While his clothes were clean, they were nearly never pressed and a razor never touched his face.

Most impressive of all Muir's traits was his search for first-hand knowledge of nature. He read what others had to say about animals and birds, lakes and rivers, forests and mountains; but he was impatient with second-hand information. He sought facts about nature, but more than facts. He pursued a life of communion with the out-of-doors.

John Muir once said a startling thing about books, and as a book lover I was shocked when I first read his statement. "I have a low opinion of books," Muir declared. "They are but piles of stones set up to show coming travelers where other minds have been, or at best signal-smokes to call attention. Cadmus and all the other inventors of letters receive a thousand-fold more credit than they deserve. No amount of word-making will ever make a single soul to know these mountains. As well seek to warm the naked and frost-bitten by lectures on caloric and pictures of flame. One day's exposure to mountains is better than cartloads of books."

Muir's low appraisal of the value of books seems out of character because he was drenched in good literature. As a boy in Scotland he had memorized all of the New Testament and much of the Old Testament. Later, as an adolescent pioneer in Wisconsin cleaning the forests, building fences, and tending to crops and livestock, he found time to pursue the study of great literature. His stern father forbade him to read in the evenings after days of hard work, telling him that he would have to read earlier if he wished to study. So the inventive young Scot devised a clock attached to a mechanism that would dump him out of bed onto the floor at an early hour. Then he studied until time to do the morning chores.

John Muir wrote and published a great many magazine articles and books, and after his death in 1914 collections of his heavy articles were published by his friends. He was a reader and writer, and his declaration "I have a low opinion of books" must be accepted as a relative statement that might well be completed with some such expression as ". . . when compared to first-hand experiences." For the second-hand experience of Nature that we get through books is a poor substitute for the direct experience of beauty in the mountains, on the lakes and high seas, on the wide-sweeping plains or under a sunset or a star-splashed sky.

The experience of nature can hardly be satisfactorily savored second hand. One must taste for himself. The great students of creation have not written books for the purpose of satisfying the reader's craving for information or to slake the reader's thirst for life's elemental beauties. Rather, their writings have been invitational, reminiscent of the prophet Isaiah's cry, "Ho, everyone that thirsteth, come ye to the waters."

The best things in life must be experienced first hand to be enjoyed. The Puritan Fathers came to North America and discovered here freedom they had never known before. They then sent word to their friends across the Atlantic, "Come, see for yourselves." Louis Pasteur found a way of combating disease, told of his findings before the French Academy of Science, and informed the distinguished and somewhat sceptical assembly that his expedition into the unexplored realm of preventive medicine was not a private enterprise for Louis Pasteur alone, nor was it an experience they could have only second hand. "Come and see for yourselves," he invited them.

A person can know all about driving a car by reading a pamphlet about it, and he can learn all the traffic and safety laws by memorizing a few simple instructions. But while knowing about driving, he is still no driver until he has had considerable experience behind the wheel of a car and until the proper habits of thinking and acting become automatic with him.

Blaise Pascal, the French mathematician, scientist, and philosopher, was at work in his laboratory soon after the death of his beloved daughter when a scientist friend stopped by to see him. Observing Pascal's faith and quiet trust in the face of his tragedy, the friend said, "Pascal, I wish I had your creed, then I would live your life." Pascal replied calmly, but firmly, "Live my life and you will soon have my creed."

The great creeds are attempts, often fumbling, to explain a way of life, just as books are endeavors to explain experiences. But creeds and books do not come first. Experience does. Whether we want to know nature, freedom, driving a car, or the goodness of God, as the Japanese proverb puts it, "One look is worth a thousand reports."

32

VARIETIES OF KNOWING

WHILE laying stone steps along the brook one June evening, we discovered to our astonishment two lady-slippers. These lovely orchids almost gave us a start — the sort of mixed feeling of surprise and wonder one has when caught off guard by a mink or a fox which silently watches a human intruder from a covert of brush. For some reason one suddenly turns, and there the animal stands, wide-eyed and still, then bounds lightly away. So with these bright wood-orchids. For how long they had stood, one on either side of the brook, I do not know. Were they there four days ago when we last visited the stream? Golden-crowned and wrapped in leafy, regal robes of green, could these beauteous members of woodland royalty have been overlooked?

Do plants, with some remote and primitive consciousness below the level of gnat or amoeba, "know" when other creatures are near them? Some are heliotropic and always turn their heads toward the sun. Some have a sense of touch and quickly close upon and trap insects that venture into their blossoms. Then could plants like lady-slippers, in ever so dim and obscure a way, feel and "know" about the near-passing of such a high-temperatured creature as a human being? Would the difference be felt — the margin of warmth between the cool breezes of the streamside and the 98.6-degree-Fahrenheit body heat of a man and a woman and a girl? Could those yellow lady-slippers, like a deer or a rabbit, have sensed our presence without our knowing of theirs?

Ordinarily we speak of knowing and not knowing as two simple absolutes, one indicating acquaintanceship with fact and the other ignorance. "Either you know it or you don't," says the teacher, catching a pupil trying to guess an answer to a question. But knowledge is not so simple a thing. It is various in kind and breadth and depth.

In recent years scientists have given much attention to the plant world and have proven that plants are far more alive than was once reported. Their responses to stimuli have some dim kinship to what we know as consciousness. Plants react to stimuli as if they possessed some deep awareness of what is going on about them. Is this awareness a kind of "knowing"? Perhaps. But if it is, such knowledge has only a remote relationship to human perception of fact, event, and method. Simple awareness, sufficient for response, begins at primitive levels, and if it is a kind of knowing, it must be the rawest, most unrefined sort.

Knowledge as acquired learning of fact or skill is of a higher type and is the kind we celebrate at high-school commencement time. It is important to the effective handling of life. If a person is to be a good member of his community and generation he must seek information about his town and his world, about the well-being of those about him and the shape of things in these times. He must know all he can about himself — his body and mind, his capacities and skills, his job, his family, his school and church and government. Knowledge of fact will always be incomplete, and for that reason one's education ought never to end.

Knowledge of fact is not necessarily good or bad, excepting as the one who has it is good or bad. We now face the possibility that our new knowledge of nuclear power can mean the end of civilization if men with unworthy ambition mismanage it. But we also possess the hope that our new knowledge can be an unequaled material blessing if men of good will are good stewards of it. Factual knowledge can transform the world into a cauldron of terror or a place of plenty, depending upon our use of it.

But knowing mere facts is insufficient. Knowing "how" as well as "what" is an essential kind of knowledge. A person who owns a good and rare violin possesses nothing but a museum piece of wood and gut unless he knows how to play it. It is reported that a certain manufacturer spent a small fortune attempting to repair a heavy-duty electric motor that suffered from frequent breakdowns. At last a renowned expert was called in. He looked the motor over carefully, made two taps with a hammer and the motor started running smoothly and without a flaw. Some days later the manufacturer received a bill for $50.00. Indignantly he sent the repairman a notice that the bill was too high and demanded an itemized accounting for the work done. By return mail the itemized account arrived and read as follows:

For tapping with hammer	$ 1.00
For knowing where to tap	49.00
	————
Total	$50.00

Knowing what you want is not enough, whether it is a smoothly running motor or a smoothly running career, an improved game of golf or chess or better marks in high school or college, or a happy marriage. You must know, too, how and where to tap. Knowing life's worthwhile goals is a good thing, but of too little consequence unless we know how to reach them.

Knowing "why" is a basic kind of knowledge, generally known as "understanding." One of the real problems of our time is that we have more learning than understanding, more facts than appreciation. Our systems of communication have been greatly expanded until we can now know what is happening in the furthermost parts of the globe within seconds after the events transpire. We know what people are doing, but our understanding has not caught up so that we can appreciate why they are doing it. Understanding is penetrating, valuable knowledge. In geometry understanding means more than reciting a theorem. It is the ability to show how earlier propositions lead to this particular proposition. In history it is the capacity to go beyond the memorization of important dates in the Civil War, such as when particular battles were fought and particular campaigns were won. Understanding is the intellectual power to trace the conditions that developed into the Civil War and the occurrences that made the loss of certain battles and the winning of others inevitable. Understanding is seeing things in terms of their connections with other things, knowing why they hang together, why they came about and what their consequences will be. To understand people means not only knowing *how* they act, but *why* they act as they do. When Mrs. Albert Einstein was asked if she understood her husband's theory of relativity, she smiled and replied, "No, I don't understand it. But what is more important to me, I understand Dr. Einstein."

Wisdom goes beyond knowing "how" and knowing "why." Wisdom is a knowledge of values. It sees possessions, such as money, as means and not ends. It draws a line between momentary pleasure and lasting joy, between tolerance and indifference, between being great and being famous, between passion and love, between service and show, between what is easy and what is right. Wisdom is intellectual and spiritual good taste when confronted by a choice, so that amidst the plenteous offerings the world makes to us of kinds of work and play, of amusement and study, of food and drink, of mates, of arts, and all the rest, we choose what will be most lastingly and most profoundly satisfying.

One of the chief problems of our times is not world-wide ignorance but a widespread inaction concerning our best knowledge. We are much like the farmer of southeast Arkansas who was approached by a book salesman about purchasing a set of books on scientific agriculture. The old gentleman thumbed his way through the volumes and then announced, "Nope, I don't want to buy them books."

"But, sir," answered the salesman, "if you had these books you could farm twice as well as you do now."

"Heck, son," replied the farmer, "I don't farm half as good as I know how now."

Is our problem that we need more knowledge or more practice?

33

THE PERIL OF STICKING TO THE FACTS

NOT long ago I purchased some highly technical books on animal life because I wanted to find out some things that the average naturalist has been unable to tell me. Some of these books remind me of the scholarly preacher who was disliked by a ten-year-old boy who found him singularly tiresome. When the youngster was questioned as to his evident discomfiture during the learned reverend's preaching, he replied, "I don't like to listen to him. He answers too many questions nobody ever asks." So with these books. They will never be best sellers. They answer too many questions about animals that virtually nobody asks.

Concerning a red squirrel for instance, its hind foot is from 40 to 57 millimeters long and its skull length from 42.9 to 48.7 millimeters. The bristly long hairs known as vibrissae, growing on the lower face of an adult female mule deer, vary from 12 to 38 millimeters in length and project at an angle of about 45 degrees above the horizontal at about 35 degrees from the longitudinal axis of the head and parallel the slant of the eye. These facts may represent some truth concerning red squirrel and deer, but they leave me somewhat unaffected. They answer questions I have never asked.

The drama of squirrel and deer life lies less in minute measurements than in the way they live and solve their problems — how they communicate with their kind; how well they hear, see, and smell; how they run and groom themselves and avoid or conquer their enemies; how they fraternize, play, rest, feel and reproduce their kind; and how they keep warm with temperatures diving far below zero. These are facts about red squirrels, deer, and other animal neighbors with which I want to become much more familiar. And then, beyond the facts, I am glad to have a deep knowing about some animals with which no statistics could compare. I know what it is to have a red squirrel treat me like a part of the forest, running up one of my arms, across my shoulders and down my other arm as I sat on a log in our woods on a wintry day. And I know what it means to have wild, spotted twin fawns stand near me, unafraid, as they browsed on apple twigs on a rain-swept late-summer afternoon at Hidden Brook.

"Let's stick to the facts," people say as they seek out the truth. But what we usually mean by "the facts" is represented by hard, bone-dry statistics, vital to the whole truth as a skeleton is to the whole person and bearing about as much resemblance! Jack Webb, who once played the part of a solemn detective on a television program, exemplified the attitude of fact-mindedness, frequently demanding of a witness, "I want the facts, man, just the facts." If Mr. Webb had gotten exactly what he asked for, his program would have been the dullest in the field of entertainment. Luckily for Mr. Webb's show, the actresses and actors ignored Mr. Webb's plea for "facts" alone and responded with anger, confusion, wonder, fear, and other elements that make for drama. Even a detective looking for material evidence of a crime — fingerprints, footprints, a gun or a knife — regards his search a failure until he finds a motive, which is a non-material things, occupying no more space than a wish and having no more weight than a dream.

(If it is argued that a motive is also a fact, the answer is that a motive is not what Americans in common, everyday speech mean by a fact. They have in mind a thing having statistical implications, usually something occupying space and having weight. It is with this limited definition of the word "fact" in mind that I write.)

Facts are wooden-headed marionettes; their behavior depends upon who pulls the strings and speaks for them. If the manipulator is stupid, the facts act and speak foolishly; but if the handler is wise, the facts speak sound sense and even profound wisdom. For instance, it is a fact that between 1947 and 1952 television sets in the homes of America increased about 10,000 per cent. If you project this figure upon the next ten years you arrive at the ridiculous conclusion that by 1969 there will be forty television sets per family. Yet projection of figures is a common statistical practice that many people accept without blinking an eye, believing it a sure way of arriving at the truth.

Again, we make our puppet facts kneel before the great god Average and serve him. Yet Average is a false god and stupid, too, feigning a wisdom it does not possess. Take a simple case of wages. The owner of a small business is reproached for paying low wages. He replies that the average worker in his plant is well paid, getting $9,766.66 per year. And he is right. But a statistical breakdown shows the wages distributed as follows:

1 plant owner	$100,000
1 secretary	2,200
10 shop workers	15,000
(or $1,500 each)	
	————
12 workers receive	$117,200

The average wage is a good one, as the owner says, $9,766.66 per year. But only the owner receives that much!

An uncommonly dull quartermaster might discover that 300 men in the army barracks wear shoes averaging size 9. Yet it would be possible for 75 of the men to wear size 7; 75 size 8; 75 size 10 and 75 size 11, with nobody at all wearing size 9! But the average size would be 9, and if 300 pairs of shoes size 9 were ordered everyone would have the wrong size! The value of averages depends upon who figures them, what the computer is trying to prove, and how the figures are handled.

Our statistic-awed generation would do well to recognize that it is perilous to "stick to the facts" if we mean by facts only those material things that can be counted, measured, and weighed.

While we have more fact-collecting apparatus than any other generation in history, our facts have not made us ap-

preciably better people. While newly found facts have poured beneficial gifts upon the twentieth-century world, they have also dropped incomparable destruction upon us, giving us devilish means for annihilating ourselves. If we stick to the facts now, being attached only to our newly found and highly efficient scientific contrivances, we are a doomed race. Our salvation will be in sticking to something bigger than our statistics and computed strength. We had better be loyal to our God and to the welfare of all mankind.

Moreover, we need to move beyond our love for more facts to a wise use of the facts already known to us. Some time ago a report appeared in the *New York Times* dealing with a United Nations investigation of economic help to Bolivia. The *Times* reported that the reason for the lack of economic progress in that South American country lay not in ignorance of what Bolivia needed, nor even in technical know-how. The great problem was that the government was unable or unwilling to act upon such knowledge as it possessed. The United Nations mission discovered that the recommendations made by experts, and going back 40 years, had collected in vast piles in Bolivian government archives. Substantially the same remedies had been recommended by all the studies, but virtually nothing had been done about any of them. Bolivians had the facts. They stuck to them. That was their trouble. It is our problem too. We know our eating and drinking habits are unhealthy, but we persist in them. We know we should get more exercise or diet but we don't do it. We know strict budgeting would help solve our financial difficulties, but we do not bother budgeting. The newspapers keep us well informed on the statistics of automobile "accidents," and the authorities have emphasized that most cripplings and deaths occurring on the highway are avoidable, but we continue to drive carelessly. We know that no war in history has been prevented by preparations for war, but we spend more for making war than we spend for making peace.

We must advance beyond our absorption in facts to an accomplishment of some worthwhile purposes with those facts. Facts are like lumber, nails, brick and mortar, shingles and sashes — not merely to be admired, but to build with. They have meaning only as they belong to some planned structure — lumber and bricks belonging in a home, medical facts belonging to the alleviation of suffering, political facts making for better government and for world order and peace.

Again, we should recognize that the most important facts are not mathematical or statistical and seldom verifiable. They are invisible and for the most part inaccessible to close and exact scrutiny. This is true with "historical facts." The big ones are not the numbers of soldiers in any army or the trajectory of the cannons, but the motives and passions of the men that prompted them to march and to fight. We do not understand military history at all if we know only the statistics of the campaigns. Why were the campaigns organized at all? Why did Rome, the French Empire; Germany, Japan, Russia, France, England and the United States do what they did? What was in the minds of their leaders? What were their thoughts, anxieties, greeds, and hopes? These matters lie beyond mathematical analysis and documentary proof. Yet they are the weightiest components of history. By "sticking to the facts" we could not understand the history of the race at all.

Again, it will pay us to see that "the facts of life" are not as important as the way we look at them and interpret them. The entire future of the world will be influenced by whether our world leaders and their followers view scientific advances as improved means of destroying enemies or serving world need. Or, see this truth applied in a more personal realm. Here are two handicapped persons, partially disabled physically. Talk to one and she "sticks to the facts" of her handicap, repeating over and over again exactly where it hurts, how many pills she consumes a day, how expensive her medicine is, who has called on her, and especially who has neglected her. The other patient interprets her trouble in the light of the good she still finds in life, the faculties she can still employ to good use, the surprising kindnesses of friends and doctors and nurses. One patient stubbornly "sticks to the facts," the other builds beauty and blessing around them.

Finally, the best things in personal life cannot be understood by factual analysis alone. "Sticking to the facts" stifles understanding. Who knows the sea better, the chemist who analyzes a test tube of sea water in his laboratory or the sailor who, with Masefield, loves

A tall ship and a star to steer her by,
And the wheel's kick and the wind's song and the white
  sail's shaking,
And a grey mist on the sea's face and a grey dawn
breaking?

Who knows a baby better, the physiologist who can describe in fairly accurate measure how much carbon, phosphorus, sodium, iron and all the rest a ten-pound baby's body contains, or the child's mother? We know more by loving than by analyzing.

Stick-to-it-iveness is a quality that is beneficial or detrimental depending upon the value of the thing to which it is attached. One can stick to his little, mean prejudices or to his low standards, and be the worse for his loyalty. Or one can be attached to one's good friends, to the beautiful, to the highest truth he knows, and above all to the God who holds all other loyalties together, and he will be the better for his loyalty.

Stick to the facts? Rather, hold true to those highest values of which the facts are but dim shadows.

34

THE USE OF TIME

HUNTING in American forests and fields was once far more a game of stealth than it is these days. More patience was needed, more cunning. The rifleman had to approach nearer his game than does his modern counterpart because his gun would not shoot as far or as accurately as today's high-priced rifles, and there was no such thing as a repeating or semi-automatic gun to give him second or third chances if he missed his target with the first shot. So the early hunter developed an unhurried attitude. Haste meant noise from which frightened game shied away. Hurry meant a wasted shot and long minutes of delay in recharging his muzzle-loader.

Most early Americans would have appreciated the saying of Rodin, the sculptor, "Slowness is beauty." They did not slaughter a great deal of game but only what they needed, and that slowly, stealthily. They did not cultivate vast sweeps of land, but small forest openings, carefully and patiently. They did not have a great, long list of friends to whom they felt social obligation, but a few friends who lived near and who would delight in unhurried fellowship at the table and fireside. They did not read many books, but if they could read at all they knew a few books thoroughly. They believed, to use Gandhi's fine phrase, "there is more to life than increasing its speed."

Some of earth's blessings come to us in profusion. God allows us many flowers at one time, hosts of friends, variety in foods. But one thing He parcels out frugally — time. Everyone, the billionaire and the beggar alike, gets only a moment at a time. Nearly everything else on earth can be accumulated, but time cannot be hoarded. People talk lightly about "saving time" and purchasing "time-saving" devices. But time cannot be literally saved and banked as money can. No one ever has two moments at once. The big question about time therefore is not "How can I save time?" but "How should I spend it?"

Consciousness of the scarcity of time makes some people hurry through their hours. They greedily gulp them down. Others, who are wiser, savor time, tasting the flavor of every moment. The difference is like that of two hungry people called to a table where food is scarce. One bolts his food and it is gone, and the effects are wholly physical and animal. The other does not rush but relishes every morsel, and the effects are both physical and spiritual, bodily pleasure being mixed with appreciation, discrimination, and gratitude.

Our forefathers used to sing an old hymn, "Take Time to Be Holy." We could well revive the hymn, or at least the principle it proclaimed. In a world chock-full of meetings, assignments, schedules and appointments, organizations to run, and social obligations to meet, time for the cultivation of faith and character seems scarce. It is not offered to us; it must be seized, wrenched from our too-full program of living. You have 168 hours in every week. Let us say you spent 56 hours of last week at work, and 56 hours is a rather liberal amount these days. If you spent eight hours of each twenty-four sleeping and dressing, that is another 56 hours out of last week. Now that left you 56 hours of last week to do other things, of which possibly 12 hours were consumed eating. You still have 44 hours left over. What did you do with them? In all the hysterical haste of last week's living did you lay aside any hours for self-improvement and helping others?

There is no sense in our saying, "I want to be a better person," and then spending no time in soul cultivation any more than there is in a young woman saying, "I want to be a nurse, but I don't want to spend any time in nursing school." We should judge a young man foolish who declared, "I want to be a scientist, but I shouldn't think it necessary to spend time in college," and we would laugh at a youngster who claimed, "I'm going to be a concert violinist, providing I don't have to waste valuable hours practicing on the violin. Just schedule some concerts for me!" But people commonly think goodness of character automatically follows wanting to be good. It does not. The inner life takes time to develop as does a fallow field that must be plowed and disked and sowed and weeded.

How can we best use our hours to become better people?

Frequently employ scattered moments of the day to think of God. Do this in addition to laying aside clusters of time for personal devotions at the beginning of the day. Link your littleness to God's greatness, your weakness to His power.

Take time for great soul-stimulating, mind-stretching books and for stirring music. Enjoy the beauties of nature, not by quick glimpses of the stars or a hasty look at a sunset, but by setting aside fifteen or twenty minutes for slow assimilation of the Creator's handiwork.

Find some secret spot to which you can retire from life's frenzied pace and reflect upon the glorious possibilities of everyday living — the opportunities for fellowship, the goals worth living for, the things worth doing, and the basic certainties and assurances that steady us.

Take time to be unselfishly useful, doing the good that no one can repay to people who may never find the time or the interest to do good to you in return. Cheer the downcast. Lend a helping hand where needed. Play with little children. See what you can do to make your community and your world better.

A New Yorker took an Oriental friend on a tour of the great metropolis. They started out on a subway train. After they had ridden for a few moments the train made a stop, and the New Yorker grabbed his Chinese friend, pulled him to the door, pushed him across the crowded platform and into a rapid transit express train. Soon they reached their destination, and the big-city man explained proudly to his visitor that by changing trains they had saved two minutes. The Chinese looked with mixed amusement and wonder at the American and quietly asked, "Now, what significant thing shall we do with the two minutes we saved?"

Well, what are we doing with the extra moments, freed of labor, that an advanced civilization has given us?

35

TIME OUT FOR CHILDREN

ONE gauge by which to measure the greatness of a person is his estimate of little children. The grown-up playboy who would rather take a long walk with his boxer dog than with his half-grown son demonstrates a character deficiency. If a man is more interested in a stable of racing horses or a breed of dogs than he is in the character of his children, he has a twisted sense of values. The man who spends more time reading the stock-market quotations than he does reading his child's textbooks thereby shows where his real treasure lies. A woman who is profoundly interested in juvenile delinquency in general but not in her own child's discourteous behavior in particular has defective insight. The mother who never allows her child to have an independent thought or commit an independent deed confuses "mother love" with abject selfishness.

But there is a touch of greatness in any person who is thrilled at the growing wonder in a four-year-old's eyes when he sees his first elephant or when he beholds a baby kangaroo peeking from its mother's pouch. No one can be entirely devoid of greatness who breathes a prayer of thanksgiving when a baby's temperature at long last falls back to 98.6 degrees. And anyone who can spend a summer's afternoon in the company of an eight-year-old child without being bored or irritated has something in common with the angels.

Americans, on the average, are indulgent parents. When the Duke of Windsor was asked some time ago what impressed him most in America, he answered, "The way American parents obey their children!" We are attentive to the needs and wishes of our youngsters. They are provided with the best food, clothing, toys, and the most expensive entertainment in the world. We give them almost anything they want — excepting

our time. Yet, it is our time that children want most, our time spent in companionship with them. Our gift of time speaks more clearly of our love and their significance than any words of endearment or verbal assurances of affection. And it is while in our company that they learn our scale of values, our philosophy of life, our sense of fair play, our spirit of service and our religious faith.

A neighbor saw a hard-working mechanic playing catch with his son one evening after work, and the neighbor called out, "Bill, aren't you tired?"

"Sure, I'm tired."

"Well, why on earth are you playing ball with your boy then?"

The dad answered, "Because I'd rather have a backache now than a heartache later on."

It is a problem to find time to spend with children, but parents must decide between solving the time problem and having problem children.

Sociologists have begun to ask, "Is the American father disappearing?" Of course, they know he is still around biologically as is evidenced by our growing population, but they fear he is becoming extinct as far as his good influences in the lives of his children are concerned. Once, when America's was an agricultural civilization and most families lived on farms, children and fathers worked together, sowing, weeding, harvesting in the fields, and doing chores around the barn. Dads and sons were apt to hunt squirrels and rabbits together to supplement meat laid away at "butchering time," and they sometimes fished together in the stream that ran across the "back forty." But since we have become an urban society, the interests of father and child have become more widely separated and companionship more rare.

Mothers, too, are having trouble maintaining a vital contact with their children. Children are still housed, fed, and clothed under the same roof where mother dwells, but mother's interests are now so many and so scattered that the affectionate security a child craves, the aching desire for attention and response, is often lacking. There is little satisfaction in earning good grades, in reading well, in learning to stand on your head, or doing anything else well, if the people you love the most are too busy to notice or too thoughtless to praise.

One night the missionary bishop Francis Xavier returned home from a day's exhausting duties and wearily prepared for bed. Before falling off to sleep he said to his assistant, "I must sleep or I shall die. No matter who comes, do not disturb me." A moment later the door to the bishop's room opened, and Francis Xavier called out to his assistant, "I made a dreadful mistake; if a child comes, awaken me."

Whether found in bishops or parents, taking time to help children is a mark of greatness.

$$36$$

FROGS AND MEN

IN spite of all the soft music of whispering snow and the cheery whistling of winter winds, there is a certain musical note that I miss on December nights. It's missing on November and October and September nights too, and even in August. And until I hear it again, Nature's symphonic orchestra will be incomplete. The certain wild and lovely note that is lacking is the piping and singing of the frogs.

Frogs that filled our balsam-scented air with song on moist warm April nights are hibernating now in deep, deathlike slumber in soil beneath the frost line and in the bottoms of shallow brooks and ponds. One autumn night when a sudden chill nipped their sensitive skins and sent their variable temperature plunging, the frogs in our neighborhood slipped cautiously into the water and made their way downward toward winter quarters. Their temperature has continued to lower, their rate of respiration has slackened, and their circulation has slowed almost to a stop. In late summer and early fall their livers became heavily stocked with glycogen, an animal starch, a material that will sustain life until kindly Spring frees the frogs from their muddy prisons. Then they will take up their stations again and fiddle and pipe and sing on many a grassy bank or lily pad or rock.

If change in temperature comes suddenly, a frog will react appropriately. If he is chilled he will seek shelter. If he jumps upon a sun-heated rock or hot pavement he will hurriedly hop off again. But if the change in temperature is slow enough a frog will seldom notice it. His temperature can be lowered almost to freezing without his showing the slightest concern, provided it happens by gradual degrees. Moreover, frogs have been placed in cold water and the fluid has been slowly heated until the water was so hot it burned their skin. But the frogs were unconcerned. Frogs seem quite alert to sudden disaster descending upon them, but unmoved by slow-gaited dangers.

We are all a little froglike. Sudden changes alert us. For the most part we avoid violent disasters. But the perils that creep upon us quietly and gradually usually escape our attention.

When a student graduates from high school or university he does not lose the benefits of education instantly. But many a person slowly, almost imperceptibly, lets slip his study and reading habits. His avid thirst for knowledge and his craving for the best become easily satisfied. The cultivation of mind slowly disappears like fields on a well-groomed farm that is sold to a lazy lout. In time, where splendid crops of high ideas grew and where budding purposes flourished weeds take over. Fences of discrimination crumble and fall, and the place is productive of little but brambles and wild thickets.

Few marriages fall apart because of a single, big, open explosion. Married people can easily guard against that. What more commonly destroys this holiest of human relationships is the gradual increase in petty discourtesies, indignities, thought-

less and selfish acts — pretty much the same things that mar any connections, but more deadly because they are committed in the greater intimacy of the home. These hideous little acts force married couples apart so slowly that they are hardly aware that they have lost each other until a crisis comes. Then they blame the crisis for their separation when all the crisis accomplished was to focus their attention on the division that had been taking place by minute degrees.

Suicide seems terrible and abhorrent when it is committed suddenly and violently with knife or rope or gun. But it is just as tragic and just as final when it is done slowly, a little at a time, with alcohol, or lack of sufficient sleep, or with a knife and fork at the table. Probably more people in America are committing suicide at the dining table by overeating than in any other way.

There is glad gospel as well as solemn warning in the way change creeps upon us and takes us unawares. Not only the worst things happen to us slowly, but the best things come to us gradually. Character is not created suddenly. Spiritual and moral fiber are formed by daily exercises and testings — discouragements exercising our determination, irritations testing our temper and patience, duties exercising our diligence, opportunity testing our insight and purpose, bereavements exercising our faith, slights and slurs testing our charity and forgiveness.

As Rufus Jones once put it, "Nobody ever quite realizes how his life is being woven day by day out of myriads of invisible threads. But, in fact, each unnoticed influence and every imperceptible tug up or down which the ordinary daily experiences furnish are silently making the life and shaping its course. The commonplace present we hardly count because we are always looking back on a past or dreaming ahead into a rosy future, which will be full of wonderful and epoch-making events. And yet, all the time, in spite of us, the future is being made out of the present, and the stuff of our future is to be what we are now weaving in."

Spiritually we are like a man going to a wise tailor to have a suit made. He may tell the tailor that he does not need to be re-measured, that he is the same size he was two years ago when he was measured for his last suit. But the tailor gets out his measuring tape and checks on all the former measurements once more and finds a half an inch has been added here, an inch has been removed over there, and three-quarters of an inch has been added elsewhere, although the customer was unaware of it. So it is with the spirit. We are easily fooled about our own measurements and easily discouraged with our spiritual thinness or bulginess. And when we enter into God's presence in prayer we are apt to sigh, "Well, here I am again. There's no change." But God, like a wise tailor, disregards our self-estimate. He again takes our measurement, and how often, altogether unaware of it, we have lost a touch of evil here and have grown a bit of spirit here and there — a bit more patience, a little extra understanding, an added inch of love.

37

WHEN LITTLE THINGS TOUCH THE HEART

LATE spring is a time of charm, when little things touch the heart. Now the world will be full of babies. Already newly hatched trout struggle valiantly against the current of the brook. Downy ducklings will soon swim contentedly in the bay. Along the marsh's edge frog's eggs are hatching into moving polka-dot clusters of tiny tadpoles, and in secret glens of the forest the first fawns of spring are delivered, wide-eyed, into a wondrous world. In spring the earth is a world of little things.

The little things of earth have an abiding attraction for human hearts. Judged by the number of ceramic figurines of baby deer I see in homes, spotted fawns must be loved by everyone. I've known many people who do not share my fondness for dogs, but I've never met a person who wasn't attracted by a month-old puppy. Many a person who hates cats loves kittens. We can put up our emotional guard against the big things, but the little ones crawl through tiny crevices and chinks and creep into our hearts.

It is that way with little deeds. We may be too proud to ask for much help when we need it or to accept it when it is offered. But, barricade ourselves as we will behind our stout independence, little deeds of helpfulness somehow manage to get through. Someone's simple act of merely being near, bringing with him a quiet kind of caring; someone else's occasional word of encouragement; another's warm, firm hand clasp, or a thank-you note finds a hospitable reception where pride might reject a greater favor. Or someone moves a mountain of trouble for us by carrying away a few small stones once a week. An elderly lady told me a while ago of the great goodness many people demonstrated when her husband passed away. But the kindness she dwelt on most and found impossible to forget was that of her nephew's wife, who wrote her a cheerful, thoughtful letter every week for many months. Those weekly letters, gentle reminders of another's care, were small things, but they made a great difference, knocking a hole in the darkness and letting a little radiance shine in.

John Henry Jowett once told of George Gissing, who was walking along a road one day when he saw a poor little lad crying as if his heart would break. He had been sent to pay a debt of sixpence and had lost the money. The man thought of the boy's family, who sorely needed the money to pay the obligation, and of their wretchedness when they discovered its loss, and he put his hand into his pocket "and wrought sixpennyworth of miracle."

How many lives around us could be changed without a colossal upheaval! A "sixpenny-worth of miracle" would turn the trick.

Isn't this the kind of miracle-performing service Jesus honored when He said that even a cup of cold water given in the name of a disciple would be rewarded? What a wonder of refreshment a drink of cold water can bring to a tired traveler, or a perspiring field worker, or a feverish patient. And a small thing like a cup of cold water does more than quench a thirst; it stirs the heart with gratitude. It is one of the little things that touch the heart.

If I were privileged to build a team of people to help God rebuild His world, I'd be happy to trade a few folks who dream about moving mountains for a good many who are willing to carry stones, because the world is moved, as the heart is, by little people who do little things in a willing, loving way.

– KOHN –

38

WATCH WHERE YOU'RE SHOOTING

OR the most part people want good things. They sincerely desire happiness, respectability and honor, worthwhile achievement in their trade or profession, and a fine family life. But they start out with high hopes for one kind of life and end up with a record of quite another sort. The best intentions are not good enough.

Again, we may intend to do nobody real harm. We are just having innocent fun in our own way, and it's nobody's business but our own. Then we discover that in a complex world such as this there are no private affairs. Everything we do or say affects someone else, soon or late, and in spite of good intentions our follies work unexpected harm. Someone has smilingly parodied Henry Wadsworth Longfellow's poem "The Arrow and the Song":

"I shot an arrow into
   the air;
It fell to earth, I
   knew not where,
Until next day, with
   wrath profound,
The man it fell on
   came around.
It did not take him
   long to tell
Exactly where that
   arrow fell.
And now I do not
   greatly care
To shoot more arrows
   into the air."

Bizarre accidents described in our daily news reports show the unintended results of simple acts. Sometimes the doer suffers for the deed. Often others do.

A Mr. J. Smith, while shaving with a straight razor, was annoyed by a fly buzzing around his head. Smith angrily struck at the fly with his razor, missed, and sliced off the tip of his nose.

Mrs. S., of Makinen, Minnesota, was in a hurry to finish her washing, so when a pin in her washing machine broke off she looked around for a substitute. She found something that seemed made to order, sawed off the end of it, and started to hammer it into the machine when the substitute pin exploded, converting Mrs. S. from washerwoman to traveling woman. She had unknowingly chosen a stick of dynamite.

Clarence B., of St. Louis, Missouri, is an excitable baseball fan and capable of considerable indignation if the game doesn't go his way. In fact, sometimes he feels "burned up." While watching a sand-lot game a few summers ago, Clarence was struck by a hard-line drive and instantly burst into flame. The batter had unintentionally clubbed a perfect bull's-eye on a pocketful of matches. The outcome? Both batter and blaze were put out.

Plymouth, Wisconsin, literally became a boom town when sixteen-year-old Robert M. shot at a sparrow perched on a farm wagon and missed the sparrow. But his shot did hit the wagon loaded with a thirteen-hundred-pound cargo of dynamite. Casualties listed: six hundred and fifty Plymouth windows, one wagon, one sparrow.

We often hit

something bigger than what we are shooting at. When the gossip hears of the damage she has done, she becomes the epitome of innocence and exclaims, "Why, it was just an innocent remark; I didn't mean any harm." Many a person has confessed to me about some evil affair he thought was "nobody else's business." "Why, I never guessed it would go that far. Had I thought it would involve and hurt so many people I wouldn't have been so foolish!" Sometimes our shots miss their mark and hit something else. Often they hit the target but ricochet and raise havoc as they glance about from one life to another.

But there is more than warning in the thought that, besides the intended results of our deeds, every act of ours has side effects that go far beyond our purposes. That can be good. We purchase corn flakes for our breakfast, desiring nothing more than something to satisfy hunger and sustain health. But in making that purchase we outreach our purpose. In driving to the store we use gasoline which profits the service-station owner and his attendant and the gasoline- and oil-re-fining industry. In patronizing the store we help support clerks, bookkeepers, grocery owners, wholesalers, truckers, farmers, farm-machinery manufacturers — all who had anything to do with those corn flakes from the time the seed was sown until they were poured into your cereal dish. Even eating breakfast cereal is not a private affair. Lives other than our own are involved. We are constantly doing more good than we know.

Olive Schreiner has said in her poem "By Our Stairs":

When we lie down worn out,
Other men will stand, young and fresh.
By steps that we have cut they will climb;
By the stairs that we have built they will mount.
At the clumsy work they will laugh;
And when the stones roll they will curse us.
But they will mount, and on our work;
They will climb, and by our stairs!
No man liveth to himself,
And no man dieth to himself.

154

Both the tragedy and the glory of life are involved in the accidental effects of our deeds — the things we do not mean to do.

39

A LOVE FOR STRANGERS

FROM our front windows at Wide Sky Harbor we see cottontail rabbits nibbling among the St.-John's-wort plants along the beach. Four hundred years ago the great grandsires of these rabbits hopped along this shore as they do now, but not one rabbit in all America had ever tasted St.-John's-wort. This plant is a foreign immigrant which the soil of this continent has accepted just as it has welcomed the Spanish Conquistadors, the Puritan fathers, the Virginia colonists, and all the rest. And now this pretty European lives in abundance along lakes and streams, in fields and at roadsides in almost every county of the Eastern states.

The tough-stemmed, yellow-flowered little visitors to these shores, the St.-John's-wort, symbolizes something of the greatness of America. This country, at its best, is warmly hospitable to strangers. This autumn the granaries of American farms are well filled with the harvested gold of foreign plants. Some of these cultivated plants originated in Europe and others in Asia, but all of our common small grains have been introduced from the Old World. Oats are natives of eastern Russia and were cultivated by the barbarian inhabitants of Europe long before the birth of Christ. Wheat, too, is a foreign import. One of the oldest of all the cultivated plants, wheat is known to have grown in the Mediterranean portions of Asia and Africa before 4,000 B.C. This grain was brought to Mexico by the Spaniards in the sixteenth century, and it was introduced to Virginia and Massachusetts by the seventeenth-century English colonists. Rye is a foreigner. It originally grew in the Mediterranean region and was cultivated and harvested by the

ancient Greeks. Probably not a grain of rye grew in America until after 1550. So with barley and millet, sugar cane and sorghum, carrots and cabbages, timothy, redtop and white clover, and many of the fruits we have on our table, they found their way to America in the baggage of immigrants from the old countries on the other side of the sea. America has been hospitable to them. Here they have grown and prospered.

America's greatness is attached to the love for foreigners which is epitomized by the inscription on the Statue of Liberty in New York Harbor:

> *Give me your tired, your poor,*
> *Your huddled masses yearning to breathe free,*
> *The wretched refuse of your teeming shore,*
> *Send these, the homeless, tempest tossed, to me:*
> *I lift my lamp beside the golden door.*

The history of this great country could not be understood or appreciated without seeing that America is magnanimous, big-hearted, with an instinctive affection for foreign plants and ideas and people.

Wherever in the life of a nation or the soul of an individual we find such hospitality toward the stranger, we know we have chanced upon greatness. Small spirits shrink from strangers. They cannot entertain a new idea nor welcome a person of different color or manner of speech or religious faith into their midst. They are overly conscious of differences. The greater the soul, the more room he can make in his heart for the outsider.

It is reported that during World War I three soldiers — one a Protestant, another a Roman Catholic, and the third a Jew — were marching together toward the thick of battle. While passing through a French village near the battle line a stray shell burst near them, instantly killing the Protestant soldier. His companions went to a nearby parish house and begged the priest to bury their fallen buddy. The priest, a kindly soul, assured the boys he would give the lad a fitting burial, but he could not inter him inside the Catholic cemetery, because that ground was consecrated for people of the Catholic faith. However, he would bury the Protestant soldier as close to the holy ground as possible. After their friend had been laid to rest the two remaining soldiers moved up into a fierce engagement with the enemy. After several weeks of bloody fighting and hair-breadth escapes from death, the two surviving buddies were granted a furlough and returned to the little village, called upon the priest, and asked him to accompany them to the final resting place of their friend. To their astonishment the priest led them inside the gate of the cemetery and to a flower-bedecked plot near the fence — but just inside. The boys thought the priest must be mistaken for they had seen the young soldier buried outside the fence. How could this be his grave? The priest, understanding their surprise, explained, "I assure you this is your friend's grave. You see, I was not allowed to move his body, but no one could stop me from moving the fence!"

Most of the time we cannot change our fellow men, converting them to our way of seeing things. They will not all come to our church, join our political party, vote our way on a referendum, or unite with us in our favorite crusade. There is one thing we can do about them, however. We can move the fences of sympathy, concern and good will to take them in.

40

WHAT IS SUCCESS?

THE LaBrea Tar Swamp within the city limits of Los Angeles, California, contains great deposits of pitch that have yielded up the bones of many species of prehistoric animals. Scientists explain that thousands of years ago wildlife from the surrounding hills and mountains came to this place, perhaps for water, and became trapped in the sticky substance underlying the pools and sank slowly to their deaths. The pitch sealed their bodies from the air, beautifully preserving their skeletons from the ravages of time. From these pits skeletons of sabre-tooth tigers, the gigantic teratornis, giant ground sloths, huge mastadons and dozens of other prehistoric creatures have been taken and exhibited at museums throughout the country.

Many of these huge creatures were predators of unimaginable strength. Their battles with each other and attacks upon smaller creatures must have shaken the earth, and the sight of them must have paralyzed the weaker animals of the forests and swamps with terror. If prehistoric man gave any thought at all to the matter, he must have concluded that these monstrous creatures would live forever. Certainly at long last they would conquer the earth. But now they are gone. Only their skeletons remain as mute witnesses to their prehistoric existence.

Mingled with the massive bones of these ancient giants, searchers have found the remains of lowly rabbits, rabbits like those that scamper through our winter-laden woods and visit our lush gardens in summer. These meek denizens of primeval swamps seem like Nature's miserable failure when compared to their primordial neighbors, the house-size mammals and lizards. But the obvious successes, the mountains of flesh and dynamos of muscular power, perished. Their age and race passed away, and the obvious failures, the humble, mild rabbits, are with us still.

The appearances of success and failure are deceptive; we cannot trust our eyes and minds. To many a mind the successful person is one who can do as he pleases, having money enough and influence enough to bend people to do his will, living above or below morality and largely apart from mercy and love. The successful person is one who dominates situations and people. But nothing *recedes* like such success, as the disappearance of the dinosaurs, which dominated a geological age, abundantly witnesses.

Billy Rose once told in his newspaper column of a meeting held in 1923 in the Edgewater Beach Hotel in Chicago. Seven of the most powerful and influential financial leaders in the world attended the gathering. It was said that these seven men controlled more wealth than there was in the entire United States Treasury. They were Arthur Cutten, greatest wheat speculator in the world; Richard Whitney, president of the New York Wheat Exchange; Albert Fall, member of the President's Cabinet; Jesse Livermore, the leading "bear" on Wall Street; Ivar Krueger, chief of the world's greatest monopoly; Charles Schwab, president of the world's largest independent steel company; and Leon Fraser, who was president of the Bank of International Settlement. What an assemblage of eminent successes! But by 1948 this is what happened to them: Cutten died abroad, insolvent; Schwab died penniless, having lived the last five years of his life on borrowed money; Livermore, Krueger, and Fraser committed suicide; Whitney spent time in Sing Sing Prison; and Fall was released from prison, ill, so that he could die at home. Nothing shrinks like material power, and nothing recedes like worldly success.

But if lasting success is not found in dominance, in accumulation of power as represented by wealth and fame, how can it be achieved? Those whose achievements have lasted and whom history has finally called "great" are not the predators and the accumulators, but the self-giving: Florence Nightingale, who gave herself to nursing; Lincoln, who gave himself for the Union and for freedom of the slaves; Beethoven, who gave the world a greater music; Shakespeare, who gave us a grander literature; and Jesus Christ, who came "that they might have

159

life and have it more abundantly." The successful are always
the givers.

I think of the strange, but true, definition of success when
I see snowshoe hares and their rabbit cousins, fed upon by
beasts and man, yet for all their self-giving, surviving the
passing of geological ages while their primitive contemporaries,
the powerful and predaceous monsters, have perished.

41

ALWAYS READY

ANY time we walk through our woods these days chickadees scatter from our path. The gem-eyed, plump little bundles of black, gray, and white feathers, loaded with energy and cheer, dart but a short distance and alight on the bare limbs of birches and populars or the needled boughs of spruce and balsam from which they chime their clear, sweet calls, "dee-dee-dee-dee, chick-a-dee-dee." They play acrobatic stunts on every tree and shrub, hanging upside down, twirling around a twig, following-the-leader through the spicy cedars, then dropping to the woods' floor to embroider a new blanket of snow with the delicate stitching of their tracks.

Among the small birds of the North chickadees are my favorites. I've often asked myself why, and I've concluded it is because of their jaunty, optimistic air, their undiscourageable resourcefulness that enables them to find a "living" where other birds fail, their companionable spirit that prompts them to be on friendly terms with other living things — the deer in the forest, the fox on the hunt, and man on his saunter over a forest trail — and the courage that enables them to face the coldest, most blustery winter the North can hurl at them. But in addition to these characteristics, I favor chickadees simply because they are always here, in every season, perpetual reminders of the beauty and wonder of all bird life, and this marvel above all others — their amazing preparation for the emergencies that will confront them in their short lives.

These chickadees, like all birds, have bills adapted to the demands of procuring and using food. In the case of the black-capped carolers of our woods the bills are sharply pointed and strong, made for prying under bark and into small crevices for insects and insect eggs.

These birds are covered with feathers, one of the strongest structures in proportion to size and weight that we can find in any organism on earth — almost weightless so as to be no burden, yet strong to support a body in rapid flight.

For the energy-consuming work of flight the chickadee, like most other birds, has a heart that is always ready to supply remote tissue of the body with freshly oxygenated blood. In proportion to the bird's weight, the heart is large and strong. While in man the heart averages less than one percent of his weight, the bird's heart is much larger proportionately. A hummingbird's heart weighs from nineteen to twenty-two percent of its total body weight. And while the average heart beat for adult men is around seventy beats per minute, and eighty for women, the heart of a sleeping black-capped chickadee beats four hundred times a minute, and twice as fast when the bird is active.

Taken feature by feature, a bird stands in strange contrast to man with all his civilized paraphernalia for making life easy, and with his accumulation of preparations for meeting life's emergencies. Resting just as it is on a frosty limb on this wintry day, the chickadee is ready for living or dying, for sleep, for feeding or for quick flight. Maybe this mixture of simplicity and readiness, this uncomplicated preparation for whatever faces it, is what charms me most about chickadees, because it hints at what life should be like.

When in school or college, we ought never to "cram" for examinations, making lengthy, frantic preparations. We should be studied up to date, having steadily reviewed the most significant subject matter in our course so that no hasty, frenzied, last-minute preparations should be necessary.

A person's devotional life should keep him "prayed up" so that when emergencies come his prayers are not an agonizing cry to a stranger-God for unaccustomed help, but an acknowledgment of a dependency upon a Power that is well known and an affirmation of trust in one's Father. A healthy devotional life is one that keeps one always ready for life's worst and its best, its gravest dangers and its most glowing opportunities.

Much of our human disquietude and

apprehension when faced with the possibility of death is understandable and natural. We do not wish to leave the ones we love, and we dislike dropping our unfinished work. But there is a great difference between wishing death could be postponed for a time and being panicked at its coming. Most terror of death stems from a feeling of unreadiness. We are not yet clean enough. We have not yet righted some wrongs we have done. There is forgiving yet to be taken care of, and forgiveness to be gained. We are not ready. A Vermont housewife demonstrated in her housekeeping a principle by which all of us might well live. When a city visitor exclaimed upon looking at her tidy rooms, "Does your house always look this neat?" she firmly replied, "Of course! I never go to bed without leaving my house in dying condition."

But a good "dying condition" means a good living condition, too. It means living so well that no matter the emergency, one is ready for it, engaging in such practices that one would not need to be ashamed to have any of them be one's last earthly act. When John Wesley was asked what he would do if he knew that he would die on a particular night, he replied that he would eat his evening meal, preach at candlelight, say his prayers, and retire to sleep — exactly what the evangelist did every night. In the face of death he would follow the established pattern of his life. Such a spirit is in keeping with George Morris's poem "My Mother's Bible,"

In teaching me the way to live
It taught me how to die.

It reflects the disposition of Bishop Thomas Ken's simple prayer,

Teach me to live, that I may dread
The grave as little as my bed.

Readiness to die and readiness to live are two sides of the same coin.

Whatever measure of peace of mind we find here on earth will be discovered somewhere in this realm of readiness for whatever comes. A farmer, needing a hired man, interviewed several prospects. One tall, muscular, bright-eyed lad greatly impressed the farmer, who thoroughly questioned the youth, at last asking him what faults he had. The young man replied, "Well, the last man I worked for complained I was terribly hard to wake up during a windstorm at night." That gave the farmer pause, but he finally decided to hire the fellow in spite of his fault. A few weeks passed, and the lad's work proved most satisfactory. But then came a night when a strong wind tortured the area, whipping the trees in the orchard, thumping on the doors and banging on the windows of the farmhouse and awakening the farmer who called his hired man so that they could check on their equipment, buildings, and livestock. But the hired man would not awaken. The farmer pounded on the lad's bedroom door, but to no avail. He entered the room and vigorously shook the youth who groaned sleepily, turned over and slumbered on. At last the farmer gave up and went out into the storm alone. To his astonishment he found that the haystack was covered with waterproof canvas anchored to the ground with tent stakes. Heavy stones weighted down the lumber pile. The doors to the barn, chicken houses, and tool sheds were all shut and locked. The farm was ready for a storm. Then the farmer knew why his hired man slept soundly during a storm at night. Sound sleep and sound living alike are possible when we keep constantly strong so that no storms can take us by surprise.

42

HIDDEN BEAUTY

ONE of America's best loved trees is the white oak, a stout and stocky tree built to withstand the shock of tempest, to wrestle with storms, and to win. A single oak in itself sometimes seems to be an entire forest. It stretches out to embrace as much earth as it can with its roots; to sift as much warm, amber sunlight as it can with its leaves; to offer as much shelter as will be welcomed by the birds of the air; and to supply as much acorn food as it possesses to foraging deer and squirrels and jays.

A white oak is loved for its majestic height and its powerful girth and the astonishing span of its limbs — qualities which can be achieved only by attaining a great age. In America there still stand venerable white oaks that are as old as our nation. When Salem, New Jersey, was founded in 1675, Quaker John Fenwick, for purposes of treaty-making, convened Indians in the shade of a great white oak that stood as a landmark. That tree still overshadows the Friends Cemetery at Salem. In the churchyard of old Saint Paul's at Fairlee, Maryland, a white oak towers 118 feet, with a spread of 127 feet, and at Wye Mills, Maryland, an old patriarch blesses earth and space with limbs that reach 148 feet in gesture of benediction. Although most of their contemporaries succumbed to the march of civilization and to the need for the oak's excellent timbers used in building blockhouses, log cabins, barns, bridges, barrels, and ships, a few monarchs still reign over groves of younger oaks, rustling their commands and in a last show of slipping strength splintering the sunshine into fragments of gold.

But besides its obvious grandeur, the white oak possesses a hidden inner beauty. Clip a twig. Cut it cleanly, and look at the light-colored pitch-wood in the center. The cross section of a twig is not round, as in most trees, but star-shaped. Besides its evident unconcealed loveliness, every white oak possesses a secret star, a hidden beauty.

This is one meaning for character in a tree, a nation, or an individual — possession of some hidden beauty comparable to, or exceeding, attractive outer appearances. A nineteenth-century sage and a twentieth-century beauty agree on the relationship between inner beauty and outward appearance: Ralph Waldo Emerson declared in his *Conduct of Life* that "there is no beautifier of complexion, or form, or behaviour like the wish to scatter joy and not pain around us," and Claudette Colbert has said, "It matters more what's *in* a woman's face than what's on it." We would be wise to examine and re-examine our modern civilization as well as our individual characters by such standards. Is the face that America shows to the world an expression of our inner interests and national ambitions? Are we having a hard time with our national appearance and with acceptance by the new nations mainly because we have in the past not sought so much to scatter joy as to flaunt our wealth and our might? Perhaps we shall *look* better to the world only after we have learned to *be* better.

Not long ago it was revealed by a beauty and fashion magazine that in America nearly nine times as much money is spent in a single year on perfume alone as is spent on medical research. And nearly fifty times as much is spent per year on shampoos and other hair preparations and on hand lotions as is invested in cancer research. We spend money through pipelines for appearances and through eye-droppers for the real, essential welfare of our people. Do we Americans care more for how we look than for what we are?

Oren Arnold has told in *Nation's Business* of an acquaintance who once wanted to be of help to a talented Navajo squaw. She was a rug and blanket weaver of rare skill. Being a religious person himself, and seeing an opportunity to edge in a bit of religious propaganda, the man requested that a rug be woven with some of the white man's religious symbols in it. When the squaw solemnly delivered the rug and received her pay, the purchaser saw how miserably he had failed as a religious propagandist. Instead of a cross, a communion chalice, or a stained-glass window, the squaw had woven into the rug pictures of automobiles and pop bottles. To her mind they represented things the white man worships. Do our outward appearances reflect our inner devotion?

Are we like a boy engaged in washing a window, expending vast energy in cleaning and polishing the outside of the glass, rubbing and rubbing to remove a stubborn smudge, only to find at last that the soiled spot is on the inside?

There is little said in the Bible that would give us a clue as to Jesus' appearance. We know nothing about His height or weight. The color of His eyes, hair, and complexion we can only guess. We do know that men, women, and children were attracted to him singly and in multitudes, but His attraction was evidently not in His unmentioned physical appearance but in His compassion, His love, His forgiveness, and His gracious words. People came to Him because of an inner beauty that the discerning were quick to find and appreciate. One little girl once pensively said to her mother, "Mom, do you know, I think Jesus was the only one who dared to live His life inside out!" His hidden beauty did not remain hidden.

One of beauty-conscious America's chief needs is for more people who will develop an inner beauty that exceeds synthetic outward good looks and who will then refuse to hide the inner splendor.

Dare we live life inside out?

43

AN EYE FOR THINGS THAT LAST

WHEREVER we find an instance of man's interest in durability and permanence, we know we have glimpsed a touch of greatness. No matter if it is a well-built stone wall or a fine job of carpentry, a solid piece of furniture, a well-constructed fence or a strongly bonded marriage, when we can say of it, "It will last for a lifetime," we feel an element of greatness is there.

Prehistoric man, sensing the fragility and brevity of life, sought some degree of permanence by leaving stone monuments as durable marks that would outlast him, informing future generations that he had once been here on the earth. Later, stone tombs and architecture were constructed, metallic sacred vessels, bracelets, and ankle rings were fashioned, and durable writing materials like papyri and stone were used so that some signs of a person's existence might be left behind.

And modern man has not lost all of this zest for durability. There is some of it in even the young. While walking down a street in a small Midwestern town one day, I came upon a group of boys who were examining a freshly laid piece of concrete. Evidently the day before they had printed their initials in the cement with their fingertips. Now they were overjoyed that their names were permanently fixed where any passer-by could see them in years to come. Just as I approached, I heard one youngster shout gleefully, "Yep! Mine's dry." The boy had found a satisfaction of permanence, leaving his mark where it would not be erased in some tomorrow.

The early-American pioneer farmer possessed an abundance of this desire for permanence. More than two hundred years ago he built stone fences that can still be seen winding through the fields and woods of New England. Even his rail fences were built to outlast the builder. His home and barn were

raised upon far heavier foundations than necessary. A traveler from Dublin, Isaac Weld, commented on the American farmer in 1798, "These people are so certain of their future that they spend a lifetime building barns for future generations." The good farmer has always had many a touch of greatness about him — a capacity for pitting his faith in the ultimate benevolence of God over against the temporary discouragements of foul weather and the occasional epidemics that took his stock; a joy and pride in creating, making with his own hands nearly everything about him — his tools, his house, his barn — and wrenching his farm out of forests and marshes; a delight in employing the power of his muscles and the wit of his mind against the stubborn resistance of nature; the patience and faith to wait for results after he has planted his seed. All these characteristic marks of greatness, and many more, the typical early farmer possessed. But as important as any other single trait was the farmer's desire for permanence and his tendency to look at his world with an eye for things that last.

Even a casual observer feels that we could well plant a bit of that spirit in our times, cultivate it, and help it grow. A standard of permanence could well replace our principle of haste. "How long will it last?" is a better question in the building trade, the tailoring trade, and in the matter of "getting religion" than the more frequently heard inquiry: "How soon can I have it?"

Permanence is of more value than appearance. In this generation we have developed an excellence of packaging. Never

171

in history have things "looked so good." But we need to balance our zest for external beauty with an enthusiasm for lasting qualities, a discrimination between packaging and product, such as the resort-town native had who commented on an overdressed resorter, "Some dream boat she is! The riggin's worth more than the hull!"

Durability would be a far better measure of worth than is our modern standard of "How much does it cost?" When a third-grade youngster proudly announced to his teacher, "We've got a new baby at our house, and it cost two hundred dollars," the teacher exclaimed, "Goodness, gracious! Isn't that an awful lot of money for just a tiny baby?" The lad replied, "Yes, it is. But think how long he will last!" Oscar Wilde once defined a cynic as "a man who knows the price of everything and the value of nothing!" If that is so, too many of us these days are cynical. The worth of a thing is more apt to be found in its durability than in its price.

Such a standard of durability as we have considered would give us a sense of stability in these times of crises and change. In the days of the French Revolution, Jean Bon St. Anare, the Vendean revolutionist, threatened a peasant, "I will have all your steeples pulled down, that you may no longer have any object by which you may be reminded of your old superstitions."

"But," answered the peasant, "you can't help leaving us the stars."

Reverence, worship, and the heart's search for God are more durable than steeples.

The best purposes for which we work outlast the money we earn while working. The influences we leave upon our fellow men survive the moments we spend with them. The spirit by which we live outlasts the flesh in which we live.

One of life's highest achievements is believing in and living for causes that survive us and doing things that outlast us.

A STREAMSIDE PRAYER

Eternal Spirit,
God of the heavens above us
And of the earth beneath our feet,
God of drifting clouds
And of leaping, laughing streams,
Hear my prayer.
As every river
Is conceived by clouds,
And every stream
Begins in rain,
So may my every thought
Come from Above
And my every purpose
Have its origin in Thee.
                    Amen

45

"PLEASE REMIND ME . . ."

Great God,
Who dost not loudly shout Thy presence,
Boast of Thy goodness,
Or roar Thy bidding at Thy children,
I thank Thee for every quiet whisper
That reminds me Thou art near
And for every plainly written memorandum
That Thy work continues in the world:
Winds softly breathing amidst green groves,
Waves throbbing against sandy shores;
Raindrops whispering to listening lawns and gardens
Quietly tell of Thy mercy and favor
And gently suggest, "Thank God."

*   *   *

Shocks of grain scrawl across the fields
A casual mention of Thy bounty.
Vegetables growing in perfect rows and
Fruits randomly strung on countles limbs
Wordlessly announce Thy grace.
The sunshine's slanting rays
Compose light-and-shadow notes that say,
"Thank Heaven!"

*   *   *

Anytime I listen,
Everywhere I look,
I am reminded God lives, and
I'm given cause for praise.

*   *   *

Because I'm absent-minded, Lord,
Please remind me

Of all that I am prone to overlook,
Of all that I so easily forget.

* * *

If self-interest should corrode my sympathies
Or self-esteem cause me to fear death,
Remind me how well the world thrived
Before I came:
Tides ebbed and swelled;
Calm followed storm;
Living things were born,
Grew, mated,
Busied themselves with their allotted tasks
And died
Without thought of me
Or need of me;
And tomorrow
And in all the morrows yet to come,
The sun will rise without my aid
And set without my help.
When I feel self-important, Lord,
Remind me.

* * *

When the day's headline news
And the smut of novels,
When bad government,
Public vice and small gossip
Bawl out noisy witness
To the meanness of man,
Then remind me that
Christ was also man
And called Himself
"The Son of man."
Remind me how much of God was once
Crammed into human flesh,
Flesh like my own,
Flesh like my neighbor's.
Remind me, Lord, remind me.

* * *

When I feel helpless
To do much about the world's vast troubles,

175

Then remind me, Lord, remind me
Of what an ordinary man can do.
Even I can help life
Another's burden that is heavier than mine.
Even I know how to live
A bit better than I'm living.
Even I can share whatever joy I have.
Even I know some words of cheer.
Even I can pray and join my weakness
To the power of God.
Although I cannot do
What I would wish,
I can do something,
And I can do it now.
Remind me, Lord, remind me.

Second Book

REFLECTIONS ON LIFE'S VALUES
AND ITS DESTINY

Part Two

LIFE'S DESTINY

46

ONE SEASON IS NOT ENOUGH

A PRIL is a great month to celebrate Easter. Now Nature reminds us that all sepulchers are sealed in vain. What the glad gospel joyfully shouts concerning Christ's resurrection long ago is secretively whispered and subtly suggested now all across the North. The cold grip of ice on Lake Charlevoix's waters is broken. On southern slopes tender shoots of grass break through the frost. The creek overflows its snow-patched bank and skips, laughing and singing, on its way to the distant lake. Bursting buds proclaim the weakness of all bonds when April comes.

This is not just another April like the last. And this spring is more than a mere continuing of last summer's old forms of life. Nature is giving birth to new creatures that have been made ready in the silent womb of winter. Spring peepers that were last year's pollywogs will soon sing from the marches. Last autumn's mummylike seeds will be this spring's sprightly flowers. Jacks-in-the-pulpit in Northern forests will preach new sermons to the greening glades. And even last month's newspapers, converted from last year's wood pulp, are transformed into this month's kites uplifted by damp breezes.

April is appropriate for Easter because the smell of thawing earth and blossoming twigs, the robin's and the thrush's call distill a rich awareness of resurrection. The splendor of April is not in prolonging the visit of last year's graces but in the miracle of *new* life.

The message of Easter is not mere immortality, the infinite prolonging of such a life as we have here. Who wants that? In my brash youth I once thought that nearly everyone hoped to live forever. But with astounding suddenness I learned how mistaken I was. Speaking informally before a group of young people in a church where I was a guest, I began the discussion with a purely rhetorical question, "How would you like to live forever?" Expecting nodding affirmative agreement, I was convinced we would begin our thought with near unanimity. To my utter amazement my question met with a chorus of resounding "No's." Besides compelling me to do some rapid reshuffling of my plans for that particular speech, the response prompted me to re-evaluate what it is that people hope will be their experience after death. Because life was, for that moment, so good that I felt it could and should go on forever was no evidence at all that everyone felt as I did, even those who were equally young.

Of course it does not take anyone long to discover that most people do not want a continued existence after death. Many would prefer utter annihilation to a further existence as they have now. They do not want their anxieties and discouragements, their proneness to sinning, their afflictions of the spirit to be stretched over an infinite future. They seek change, not continuance. What man hopes for and what the Christian faith proclaims is not prolonged existence but resurrection into a better life. In this spirit Ben Franklin composed an epitaph to be engraved upon his tombstone. It reads:

The Body
of
Benjamin Franklin, Printer
(Like the cover of an old book,
its contents torn out,
And stript of its lettering and gilding)
Lies food for worms.
Yet the work itself shall not be lost,
For it will (as he believed) appear once more,
In a new
And more beautiful edition
Corrected and Amended
by
THE AUTHOR

Mere immortality is not enough. We want to live on only if we can live better. And it is an eternal life of fulfillment and growth that makes sense to us rather than either non-existence or simply continued existence. To know that last year's seeds are fulfilled in this year's flowers, that last spring's inch-long rainbow parr will be this spring's fingerling trout, that last summer's fledgling tanagers will be this summer's nest-builders, and then to believe that the destiny of man is death without fulfillment of its latent God-given possibilities is to see the universe as extremely silly. Such a universe would complete its lesser creatures and throw away its masterpieces half done.

181

There is much within man that requires more than one season's growth, much that needs transplating into a roomier, more beneficent climate. Our imperfect understandings of each other need another life, a tenderer atmosphere, for their perfecting. Here on earth the full capacity of man's mind is never used. We "know in part" and struggle toward a perfection never reached. Our charity is inconstant and fragmentary and needs maturing toward constancy and inclusiveness. The English poet William Cowper, in appreciation of a great friendship, wrote to Hesketh, "You must know that I should not love you half so much did I not know that you would be my friend for all eternity. There is not room for friendship to unfold itself in such a little nook of life as this." Nor is there time for any of the best that is within us to come to full flowering. It is clear that we do not want to live forever — if we must live cooped up like this. If immortality were but the continuation of this life as it is, like an unborn child that could not be delivered to life in the outer world and yet could not die, it would be frustration rather than fulfillment, and the prospect would be full of dread rather than blessing.

Our hope is not in immortality — mere undyingness — but in resurrection; not in continuance of this life, but in a better life to come. Thank God, this season is not last season all over again, but a new chance for the world; and eternity is not simply this life infinitely prolonged, but resurrection.

In the moving picture *The Life of Zola* there is a court scene drenched with meaning. Emil Zola, defending Captain Dreyfus, was fighting to reopen the case of the unjustly accused and convicted army ·officer. But Zola's evidence was not admitted to court and the witnesses he had summoned were not permitted to testify. At last the judge declared the case was closed. As the friends of Dreyfus were leaving the courtroom, the lawyer for the defense pointed to a mural behind the judge's bench. It was a painting of Christ hanging on His cross. The lawyer declared, "That, too, was once regarded as a 'closed case.'"

We tenderly lay away our loved ones, and say the "final Amen." But is it final?

We come to the end of our days here, incomplete in knowledge and understanding, still not all that we ought

182

or long to be, still far short of the "measure of the stature of the fullness of Christ." Are we finished?

As winter seals the North and apparently puts an end to all the verdant things of earth, long ago a stone was rolled across the doorway of a tomb. The case was closed. But was it?

47

WHERE THERE'S DEATH THERE'S HOPE

FTER our family made our nightly deer count this evening, seeing eleven deer along the Camp Charlevoix road, we returned home, and I took a stroll up the west trail at Wide Sky Harbor.

In the somber blue-grey hour between seven and eight on this moist spring night the patches of earth exposed by the thaw present a picture of mixed life and death. There lie the twigs and limbs broken from birches and poplars, spruce and balsam by last winter's snow and ice. There rest last autumn's leaves, having danced their last fling, now moldering in dark brown heaps. Faded grasses, sprawled in soggy limpness, will never rise again. A graveyard sobriety lies thick upon the land on this last day of March.

But life is there too, not yet apparent, but life about to be born. One can feel its heart beat in the belly of Mother Earth, heavy with her young. Faint stirrings of bulbs and roots can be sensed, the first feeble quiverings of unseen organisms in small pools and rivulets, the smoldering desire of underground shoots and seeds to reach the light. Death and resurrection are commingled here.

Why is it that we think of life and death as the antithesis of each other? In nature death is not so much the enemy of life as its friend. They belong to each other and are companionable. Wherever we find an abundance of life there is also an abundance of death. Mixed with the multitude of infant grasses just now greening are the countless dead grasses. They have made way for the next generation and their decay will fertilize the soil, providing nutriment for generations of grasses yet to come.

Life and death exist in cordial communion in our streams and lakes. Fish eggs are laid in astounding profusion, but this

184

is because the mortal-
ity rate of fish eggs
and fish fry is ex-
tremely high. Only
by great reproductiv-
ity are the hazards of
life for fish overcome
enough to insure the
survival of their race.
A mature female
brook trout may lay
as many as five thou-
sand eggs in a single
season. But not all of
these eggs will hatch.
And not all that
hatch will live more
than a few hours be-
fore being gobbled
by their enemies.
Perhaps no more than

a couple of dozen will attain maturity and reproduce. The sturgeon may cast over two million eggs at a time, and so may the
halibut, and a cod has been known to lay over nine million eggs.
But life for young sturgeon in the great lakes and rivers and
for halibut and cod in the seas is even more hazardous than
for brook trout. Because death is more abundant, so must life
be more prolific.

Our near neighbor, the cottontail rabbit, may breed as
many as four times a year and produce up to seven young
each time. The young in their turn may breed when but
six months of age. If all cottontails would live out their natural
life expectancy of eight years the country would be inundated
by a flood of rabbits. But, no danger; foxes, weasels, mink,
bobcats, hawks, owls, man, and a host of other predators will
thin their ranks so that the rabbit population of these acres two
hundred years from now will not likely be more than that
of this year or year after next.

A common weed, *Sisymbrium sophia*, produces three quarters of a million seeds. It has been estimated that if all the
seeds sprouted, grew to maturity, and reproduced, the entire

185

land surface of the earth would be covered with the offspring within three years. But because death is as abundant as life no such calamity results.

Thomas Huxley once reckoned that if all the descendants of a single greenfly lived and multiplied, at the end of the first summer they would outweigh the population of China. But a scant number will live more than a few hours.

Often we hear the exclamation: "Where there's life, there's hope." In the natural world the opposite is just as true — "Where there's *death* there's hope." Without it there would be no room on earth for future generations. The world would have been crammed to overflowing with primitive forms of life within a short time after its creation. And those forms that did exist would be warped by age, worn out and, shortly the earth would have crawled .with weakened and infirm forms that had no possibility of release from their weaknesses. Nor would there be room for replacements.

Death is not in itself a sad thing, but necessary and good. The transience of life is essential to the well-being of the earth and its children.

This feeling about the bright aspect of death is more than a detached consideration of a principle of natural history. It is deeply personal, sensed with a quiet wonder and profound gratitude. It would have been no tragedy if I had never been born. But it would be a personal calamity if I could never die, if I had to hold onto the accrued debits of flesh and mind for time without end, and if I could not at last give up my place here to some new-born child who might make the world some contribution beyond my power to give.

The same kindly Creator who made life made death. And I'm uncertain as to which act shows more of His greatness, wisdom, and mercy.

48

FARTHER ON

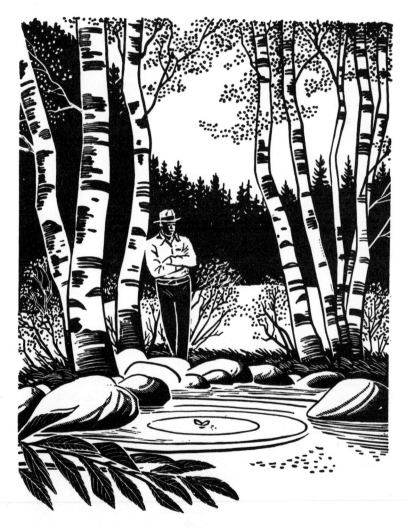

USUALLY when I take a walk along the tumbling stream at Hidden Brook or along the sandy beach at Wide Sky Harbor, every few feet I think, "I must stop now and return to the house and my duties." But then a glimpse of some inviting object up ahead draws me on. What elfin creature was that vanishing among the stream-side rocks? What new shrub sprouts from amidst the cedars? What tracks are those in the sand? What kind of wild flower peeps through the ferns at me? And I go farther on my way.

Thus it is with life. Carefree childhood or vibrant youth, mature middle-life or serene and venerable old age — any one of these would make a good stopping place, each having its peculiar enjoyments, but we are drawn inexorably on to the next stage of living and its unique adventures.

So it is with death. Death is the invitation God gives us to go farther on, where there is still greater beauty to behold, still deeper mystery to be solved, still greater fellowship to be enjoyed, a still greater height to climb.

Death is an invitation to go farther on.

49

WHAT IS BEYOND?

ANY day now male redwing blackbirds will return from their winter resorts in the South and fill the damp, spring-laden air of the marshes with their rich, vigorous song, "con-ka-ree, o-rak-a-ree." Soon thereafter the more somber females will come trooping in, settling in the lowlands, pairing off with the proud males who will show them extravagant attention and strut before them in their best dress-uniforms of shining black decorated with yellow-edged scarlet shoulder epaulets.

Amid sheltering sedges and low bushes they will build their nests of cattail fibers and woven grasses. There the gay, solicitous males will stand guard against thieving crows and marauding mink and weasels, scolding any enemy who shows his face and diving in courageous assault upon any one that comes too near. And there four or five pale-blue eggs will hatch in less than a fortnight after being laid, presenting to the shadowy world of sedges, cattails, lilies, and gently tossing water several small, vital, pulsing clumps of life.

We are fortunate that Easter comes in springtime, for now our awareness of the resurrection is reinforced by every living thing: the return of migrating birds to their summer haunts, the budding and leafing of shrubs and trees, the slow greening of the good earth, and the shy, hesitant smile that steals across sullen winter skies. Earth lays off her white woolen scarf and shows the color of her spring dress, patterned with tulips, arbutus and violets. But amidst all this resurrection the most hopeful symbol is that smooth, lustrous, primordial form of life, the egg, which holds in its thin shell the mystery of existence and the yet undisclosed riddle of the future.

An egg appears to be only a dead, naked shell, but then the miracle of life bursts through deceitful appearances, and a feathered morsel of vitality tumbles forth, like a soul loosened from the bonds of mortality. It was probably this parable of the egg that prompted Christians to adopt it as a symbol of Easter, borrowing it from their pagan neighbors, who merely

189

exchanged baskets of eggs each springtime as gestures of good will.

But more important to my mind is another lesson of the egg. The shell of an egg represents the limitation of our knowledge and understanding. Behind that calcium wall faintly stirs an embryo that is getting ready for something far greater, vaster, more wonderful than it could guess, even if its infant intelligence were magnified a millionfold. Eyes are developing to see light of which the baby bird has no conception and to behold sights which are wholly outside its tiny range of experience. Feather-covered ears are growing that will register sounds thus far unheard. Wings are budding and unfolding that will soon cleave marsh breezes and carry the freed bird over sky roads yet unvisited, on missions yet unguessed, with companions yet unknown. An egg reminds us of two kinds of life — that of preparation and that of final fulfillment, two forms of life that are continuous and yet different, bound together by one significant meaning: both lives are fashioned by the same Creator, and both are in His capable hands.

As for me, that is the persistent answer my faith offers concerning the mysteries of the Beyond. What do I know about the life on the other side of that shell called "death"? Very little. But I am certain that the God who made this life made the next, and He is there as well as here.

Dr. John Baillie, once Principal of New College in Edinburgh, has told that a man in his last illness was discussing the imminence of death with his doctor. He asked the physician what he supposed the Hereafter might be like. The man of science said there was no way of describing the future life in detail because foreknowledge is so limited. Just then the physician's dog, which sometimes accompanied him on his rounds, scratched at the patient's door, begging to get in. The doctor told the patient that the faithful dog could know nothing of what was in that room, but he knew his master was there. "Isn't that the way it is with you?" the physician asked. "You do not know all that lies beyond the door, but you know your Master is there."

What we now know about the life beyond is meager in detail but immense in value. God is there. And wherever God is, there is Heaven.